GAMES, TRICKS AND PUZZLES THAT INVOLVE YOU IN COMPETITION WITH ONE OR MORE PLAYERS— OR WITH YOURSELF

This book is dedicated to the pleasure principle for every owner of a pocket calculator. It is the product of the spirit of play being combined with the new powers that the calculator gives us—the pure joy of setting mathematics in seemingly miraculous motion, and using numbers in previously undreamed of ways.

Whether you want to amuse yourself or astound others, work out intriguing problems or play thrilling games, all you need is your own electronic marvel, the calculator, and this great new book—

THE CALCULATOR GAME BOOK FOR KIDS OF ALL AGES

ARLENE HARTMAN received her M.Ed. from Indiana University of Pennsylvania, where she majored in mathematics. A teacher of mathematics for ten years in the Gateway School District, Pa., she is currently Mathematics Consultant for the Paramus Public Schools.

More Game Books from SIGNET

THE CALCULATOR GAME BOOK FOR KIDS OF ALL AGES

by

Arlene Hartman

WITH A PREFACE BY
Dr. E. Glenadine Gibb

A SIGNET BOOK
NEW AMERICAN LIBRARY
TIMES MIRROR

I would like to dedicate this book to my mother, who first got me interested in puzzles and games of all types, and to my husband, without whose patience and encouragement it could not have been written.

NAL BOOKS ARE AVAILABLE AT QUANTITY DISCOUNTS WHEN USED TO PROMOTE PRODUCTS OR SERVICES. FOR INFORMATION PLEASE WRITE TO PREMIUM MARKETING DIVISION, THE NEW AMERICAN LIBRARY, INC., 1633 BROADWAY, NEW YORK, NEW YORK 10019.

SIGNET, SIGNET CLASSICS, MENTOR, PLUME, MERIDIAN AND NAL BOOKS are published by The New American Library, Inc., 1633 Broadway, New York, New York 10019

First Signet Printing, March, 1977

6 7 8 9 10 11 12 13

Printed in Canada

Contents

Preface

Many teachers, school administrators, and parents find themselves faced with decisions concerning the use of the hand-held or pocket calculator both in the school classroom and at home. Of basic concern is the possibility that the child or youth will not develop his own proficiency in computational skill. Consequently, some fear, the student will become solely dependent upon these electronic devices for even the simplest of mathematical computations.

One cannot dismiss this concern lightly. Such a possibility can be a reality if students are encouraged or programmed to use calculators with little or no understanding of what the calculator is doing for them. Furthermore, they may be unable to make judgments with respect to the accuracy of the results reported. Like any teaching aid or educational device, the calculator can create more problems then it can solve if misused. It should not be regarded as a substitute for pencil-paper or mental skills in mathematics. On the other hand, after understandings have been abstracted and sufficient skill has been developed in using these basic understandings, effective use can establish the calculator as a valuable device for learning mathematics both in the classroom and at home.

The National Council of Teachers of Mathematics, the world's largest organization of teachers of school mathematics, supports the position that mini-calculators can be effectively and creatively used as instructional aids to stimulate students' thinking in mathematics. I personally support this position and am pleased to write this preface for a book that has attempted to provide guidance in effective and creative uses of the pocket calculator.

Effective and creative uses can include checking answers, debugging problems, checking knowledge of basic facts, assessing insight of mathematical processes, exploring relationships, solving problems, generating number patterns, and even making the calculator "speak." As teachers and parents seeking to guide youngsters in mathematical adventures that are creative and thought-provoking experiences, more specific suggestions are helpful to us.

I express my sincere thanks to Arlene Hartman for coming to the assistance of teachers and parents alike, including teachers of teachers. This book is an especially welcomed resource. Even more important, she has opened the doors for independent explorations in mathematics on the part of children and youth themselves. The many learning opportunities provided in this book can be expected to stimulate both individual and group exploration into many mathematical concepts, especially for its intended audience—youngsters in the upper elementary and secondary schools. Also, I think that many adults can expect to find these experiences a challenging, fascinating, and productive use of a few moments of leisure time.

Whether you are a teacher, administrator, parent, or student, you are about to engage in an exciting venture into mathematics with the assistance of your pocket calculator. Personal experience plays a great role in the learning process for each of us.

E. GLENADINE GIBB
President, NCTM, 1974–76
  and
Professor of Mathematics Education
The University of Texas at Austin

Introduction

Recently, there have been a number of books about pocket calculators. Some of these books focus on number "tricks" and "gimmicks," while others concentrate only on games, and still others try to tell you all about how to use your pocket calculator. This book is not like those.

First, I must tell you that I'm a great believer in fun. Also, I'm a mathematics teacher and program coordinator. I mention this here at the very beginning of this book because I don't see why a person can't have good, challenging fun—and also learn something from the experience. There's no reason for learning to be dull and painful, and no reason for fun to be mindless and useless. So, whether you are a student who enjoys mathematics and would like to use the activities to enhance your mathematics skills, or someone who prefers to enjoy the games and tricks just for the fun they provide, by yourself or with your friends, you'll find that this book was designed for you.

There are several general features to notice before you begin. First, within each chapter the various activities are arranged from easier to more difficult. You can use some of the easier ones as a warm-up, moving to the more difficult when you feel ready. As a guide, each activity contains a suggested grade span. These suggestions, however, are merely an indication of the grade or grades in which the basic mathematics used in the activity might normally appear in a mathematics curriculum. You should not be discouraged from trying activities above your grade level, nor should you think that all activities below your grade level are too easy to be fun for you. Any trick or game which is new to you will be fun, regardless of your age or grade. And I encourage you to try some activities above your grade level—you may be surprised at how well you do.

Second, activities suggested for lower grade levels are written and organized in a manner easier for younger readers to understand. As activities move to higher grade levels, directions and examples become more sophisticated. However, a large percentage of activities, even the simplest, also contain a challenging "brain-stretcher," which should be intriguing for all ages to try, and which should give you ideas for creating more games or challenges on your own.

Third, answers are given at the end of each chapter for all parts of each activity which cannot be found directly with the calculator. This allows you to check your work as you progress through the book. Also, some activities in later chapters are related to those in earlier chapters, so checking your accuracy is important in success with later activities. And, if you're like me, you will like the assurance of seeing that you did get the right answer!

Fourth, the book is divided into two major sections to enhance the variety. Section I is devoted to what might be referred to as number "tricks," although each of them works because it is based on a mathematical concept. Each of the seven chapters in this section focuses on a specific mathematical operation or type of numeral. Some you will enjoy on your own, while others you will want to try with friends. Section II is a collection of games organized in three chapters.

And finally, there's an index at the end of the book which lists all games and tricks by grade level.

Let's look now at some of the specific contents of these sections.

The first chapter of the book—"Mix and Match"—provides enjoyable warm-up activities to get you into the spirit of having fun with your calculator. You will find many "tricks" which you can use to baffle and impress your friends. It's a good idea to practice these on your own until you master the technique; then try them out on a friend. But of course, they will be fun even if you don't get a chance to try them on your friends! The other activities in this chapter will amaze you because of the unusual, unexpected results.

As the title might suggest, each of the activities in this chapter involves at least two of the four basic operations with whole numbers: addition, subtraction, multiplication, and division. Most of them are easy enough numbers for all ages to be able to do, but many of the "brain-stretchers" in this chapter, different from most of the others in the book, involve knowledge of algebra. So, if you are advanced enough to be familiar with algebraic notation, you should find them especially challenging. Those "brain-stretchers" which do not require algebraic proofs will be intriguing for other readers. If you do attempt some of the proofs, check the answer section for the first few to see if you are on the right track.

Chapter 2 is entitled "It All Adds Up." As you might guess, this chapter focuses on "tricks" which involve only the addition of whole numbers, and I think you will be surprised at the variety of things that can be done with just this simple operation. The first several activities, although they involve relatively simple addition, should be mathematical twists which are new to most readers. Of special interest are some of the more difficult activities toward the end of the chapter which will introduce you to several mathematical ideas first introduced by famous mathematicians of earlier centuries.

"Take It Away!" gives the clue that Chapter 3 focuses on subtraction of whole numbers, although a few of the activities may also involve some simple addition. Again, the tricks range from those involving very simple subtraction to some more intricate activities. Two new wrinkles introduced include the magic squares and cubes at the easier levels, and tricks with negative numbers in the more difficult activities. This is the first time in the book you will encounter negative numbers. Whether or not you have worked with them before, you should find these activities a real challenge.

Chapter 4, "Multiplication Magic," has a series of

activities you have not encountered in earlier chapters. Many of them contain a list of multiplication problems which have a distinctive pattern in the products. You will probably find yourself predicting results after two or three examples in each, then using the calculator only to check your predictions. As you progress through these, your ability to predict should get better. Also, many of these same pattern activities will show you some shortcuts for mental multiplication which may be new to you. Two activities show you different ways early civilizations did multiplication, as well as an activity to show the way in which computers now multiply. And, as with the earlier chapters, there are a few tricks to try on friends.

For the most part "Divide and Conquer," Chapter 5, involves some basic division activities, several of which were designed to show how you can check whether or not a large number is divisible by one of the basic numbers (3, 4, 6, 7, 8, 9, and 11) without actually dividing. Using your calculator in these activities will help you discover the tricks. Afterward, the calculator can be used merely to double-check your prediction.

Through this portion of Section I all of the activities (except for a few with negative numbers in the chapter on subtraction) have involved only whole numbers. As we move to the final two chapters in this section, new sets of numbers will be introduced.

Fractions, decimals, and percents are the focus of Chapter 6, entitled "Get the Point?" One of the most intriguing of numerals, the repeating decimals (for example, .121212 . . .) are introduced here, moving from simple patterns of converting fractions to their decimal equivalents to more difficult work with these decimals. Some of the new ideas introduced in earlier chapters with whole numbers are extended here for decimals. Also, if you've moved through the earlier chapters in order, the "magic" of the numbers near powers of ten (9, 99, 11, 101, etc.) which you encountered there is reinforced here. These are also extended to the "magic" decimal numerals of .9 and 1.1. By the time you've finished this chapter, you'll be amazed at how closely the decimals parallel the whole numbers.

The most versatile chapter of this section is "X-Tensions," Chapter 7. It contains a variety of operations and numbers not covered by any of the earlier chapters, which have a more specific focus. New concepts, operations and numbers introduced include a variety of activities involving powers (largely squaring and cubing), techniques for finding square roots without using the square-root key of your calculator (if you have one), factorials, geometry, and some algebraic extensions, including more work with negative numbers. As with Chapter 1, several of the "brain-stretchers" involve algebraic proof for those familiar with it; others can be attempted by all readers. Readers interested in exploring simple beginning concepts of the calculus should be interested in trying the two activities entitled "This Is the Limit!" and "Lower Bounds."

This takes us to the end of Section I. I hope your experiences with the activities in this section will stimulate your interest in exploring and enjoying more mathematics, and I think you'll find there are many more "tricks" and challenges which haven't been touched upon in this book at all.

But in the meantime, you can relax and get ready to enjoy Section II.

Section II begins with Chapter 8, "Solitaires." As you might guess from the title, each of these activities is a game designed for you as an individual "gamester." Most of them require only one calculator; in a few cases simple additional materials, such as dice or cards, are required. When extra materials are necessary, they're listed at the beginning of each game.

There are two basic types of games in this chapter. The first is perhaps more like the "pure" definition of game where there is a "win" attained by reaching a specified goal. Those activities which fall into this category usually have only an incidental use of the calculator. The second type included here is the game-puzzle. Here, you are pitting your skill against a puzzle, using the calculator to assist in getting (and checking) the correct solution. At first glance, these puzzles may seem similar to the tricks you did in Section I. However, they are very different, because you must use your ingenuity to find the solutions, instead of following specific steps.

Those of you who especially enjoy games and puzzles with words will be particularly interested in some of the special features in this chapter. The use of the calculator "flip" to change the numeral display to letters and words (first introduced in Chapter 1) is expanded here in some intriguing logic puzzles. There are also three crossword puzzles which you first try without the calculator, using calculator problems to help you get missing letters or words, if necessary.

Chapter 9, "One on One," contains a variety of games which you and a friend can enjoy with your calculators. Many require only one calculator, but a few need at least one for each of you. As with the preceding chapter, several games also require additional simple materials.

All games in this chapter are of the pure variety, having a set of rules to follow and a definite winner. In addition to the fun you can have just in playing the games, you can enjoy the challenge of trying to find winning strategies. Many of the games also have one or more suggested variations, almost like having another new game to play! Games #13 and #14 can also be adapted so that more than two can play, adding to enjoyment with a group of friends.

The short answer section for this chapter describes the winning strategy for each basic game (if it has one). To be fair to any friend with whom you'll be playing, don't peek at the strategy, but try to figure it out yourself. And when both of you know the winning strategy for the basic game, you can try to figure it out for each variation. Winning strategies for the variations are not given to make it more of a challenge for you.

The tenth and final chapter, aptly entitled "Three or More," is another collection of "pure" games, this time designed for three or more players. For most, a maximum of six is recommended, though it's not absolutely essential.

As with both earlier game chapters, games are arranged in increasing order of difficulty. Also, several new features of game-playing are introduced in this chapter. For example, in "Name the Nominee," a game which has four rounds of partial winners before a final winner is determined, you can negotiate with other players to get more points than your delegate total allots to you. In "Override the Veto," players team up to form a winning coalition. A complex version of a bingo game also appears.

Because all of these games depend primarily on luck, although some decision-making skill is involved in several, there is no simple winning strategy for them. Obviously, some good choices can be made, where choice is available to the players. I leave it to you to determine these.

At this point we have come to the end of a long voyage together and I hope you have enjoyed the trip. Remember that we have just scratched the surface of the possibilities available with the calculators. (For teachers and parents interested in exploring the use of this book as a useful adjunct to the mathematics curriculum, a separate guide to instruction will be available, containing a variety of tips for large and small group use, as well as in learning centers.) There are many more mathematics "tricks" and games which can be created. You may well have already devised some.

I would just like to add that I have tried to create a book that has something for every reader, regardless of age, mathematics background, and special kind of interest. Whether you are a student, teacher, parent, or just plain lover of challenging fun, this book will be a good starting point for getting more pleasure (and, maybe, more learning) from your calculator. Truly, it is intended for "kids of all ages."

—ARLENE HARTMAN

SECTION I

Tricks, Teasers, and Brain-Stretchers

Chapter 1

Mix and Match

IMPORTANT REMINDER: *The Suggested Grade Span which appears in almost all "tricks" and "games" throughout the book is intended merely to show the grade(s) in which the basic mathematics involved in the problem would appear. Some students in grades lower than those indicated may also be able to do work listed at a higher grade. Also, most contain "brain-stretchers" which may also appeal to a higher grade/age level. And people of all ages should enjoy any which are new to them!*

The first group of "tricks" in this chapter is coded as for grades 4 and up. This is because the computational skills involved do not extend beyond the capability and curriculum of grade 4, but the interest level can apply to any grade/age if the reader has not seen the "trick" before.

1. Back to the Beginning SUGGESTED GRADE SPAN—4 AND UP

Do this trick with a friend, letting him do the work on the calculator.

1. Have him enter any number (4-digit is suggested) in the calculator.
2. Multiply by 2.
3. Add 4.
4. Multiply by 5.
5. Add 12.
6. Multiply by 10.

    7. Subtract 320.

    8. Take the calculator back from your friend. Remove all final zeroes by dividing by 10, 100, or other necessary power of 10. (You can do this by dividing by 10 repeatedly until all final zeroes are removed.) Show the result to your friend— the number he/she started with!

2. Turning up 23   SUGGESTED GRADE SPAN—4 AND UP

Do the same thing with this trick.

    1. Have your friend select any number (4-digit is suggested) and enter it in the calculator.

    2. Add 25.

    3. Multiply by 2.

    4. Subtract 4.

    5. Divide by 2.

    6. Subtract the original number.

    7. Now surprise your friend by telling the result: 23!

Brain-stretcher! Show why the result must always be 23.*

3. Serendipitous 60   SUGGESTED GRADE SPAN—4 AND UP

    1. Enter any 2-digit number.

    2. Add 10.

    3. Multiply by 2.

    4. Add 100.

    5. Divide by 2.

    6. Subtract the original number.

---

* In most cases in this chapter the "brain-stretcher" which asks the reader to show why a result occurs requires some knowledge of simple algebra.

What do you notice about the result each time?

Can you create a similar problem for 3-digit numbers?

Brain-stretcher! Show why the result is always what it is.

4. **Baffling Birthday**   SUGGESTED GRADE
SPAN—4 AND UP

This is a good trick to use with a friend whose birthday or age you don't know. Tell your friend to follow the directions below with the calculator, and you will tell him/her in what month he/she was born and how old he/she is. The example below is for an August birthday and 33 years old.

Directions	Example
1. Enter the number of the month.	8
2. Multiply by 10.	80
3. Add 20.	100
4. Multiply by 10.	1000
5. Add 165.	1165
6. Add your age. (33)	1198
7. Now take the calculator back from your friend, and without showing him/her what you are doing, subtract 365.	833

The last two digits (33 in the example) are your friend's age. The first digit or digits (8) is the number of the month in which your friend was born.

You'll have to be careful if your friend is less than 10. Then only the last digit is the age.

Brain-stretcher! Show why this trick works.

5. Two for the Price of One

SUGGESTED GRADE
SPAN—4 AND UP

Here is another trick you can use to fool your friends.

Directions	*Example*
1. Have your friend pick two 1-digit numbers, but not tell you what they are.	7, 9
2. Tell him to enter the first.	7
3. Multiply by 5.	35
4. Add 3.	38
5. Multiply by 2.	76
6. Add the second number.	85
7. Now take the calculator back from your friend, and without showing him what you are doing, subtract 6.	79

Of course, the first digit of the answer is your friend's first number and the second is his second number.

Brain-stretcher! Show why this works.

6. Calendar Contortion

SUGGESTED GRADE
SPAN—4 AND UP

This is an interesting trick that works with a calendar. You can use a copy of the one below, or pick the month it now is for you.

MARCH						1977
		1	2	3	4	5
6	7	8	9	10	11	12
13	14	15	16	17	18	19
20	21	22	23	24	25	26
27	28	29	30	31		

Directions	*Example*
1. Put a square around any set of 9 dates.	
2. Enter the smallest number of that square.	9
3. Add 8.	17
4. Multiply by 9. Remember your answer.	153
5. Clear. Add all 9 numbers in the square (9 + 10 + 11 + 16 + 17 + 18 + 23 + 24 + 25)	153

Try this with several different squares in the same month or with different months. Does it always work?

Brain-stretcher! Can you explain this or prove it?

7. Back to the Beginning B

SUGGESTED GRADE
SPAN—4 AND UP

You can do this with a friend or on your own.

1. Select any 2-digit number.
2. Multiply by 2.
3. Add 4.
4. Multiply by 5.
5. Add 12.
6. Multiply by 10.
7. Subtract 320.
8. Divide by 100.

What happens every time? Try several numbers to be sure.

Brain-stretcher! Show why this happens.

8. Turning up 10   SUGGESTED GRADE SPAN—4 AND UP

1. Enter any number.
2. Multiply by 6.
3. Add 48.
4. Multiply by 5.
5. Add 60.
6. Divide by 30.
7. Subtract the original number you first entered.

Do this for several different original numbers. What always happens?

Brain-stretcher! Can you show why this always happens?

9. Back to the Beginning C   SUGGESTED GRADE SPAN—4 AND UP

1. Enter any number.
2. Multiply by 3.
3. Add 30.
4. Multiply by 5.
5. Add 600.
6. Divide by 15.
7. Subtract 50.

Do this for several numbers. What always happens?

Brain-stretcher! Can you show why this always happens?

10. More Calendar Contortions   SUGGESTED GRADE SPAN—4 AND UP

Here is another calendar number trick. Use the calendar below, or use one from the current month.

MARCH						1977
		1	2	3	4	5
6	7	⑧	9	10	11	12
⑬	14	15	16	17	18	19
20	21	22	㉓	24	25	26
27	㉘	29	30	31		

Directions	*Example*

1. Put a square around 16 dates.
2. Add the two numbers in opposite corners (6 + 30 or 9 + 27).   36
3. Multiply by 2. Remember the result.   72
4. Circle 4 numbers in the square so that each circle is in only one row and one column.
5. Add those 4 numbers: 13 + 28 + 8 + 23 =   72

This should always give the same numbers in step 3 and step 5 if you do it correctly. Try it with different circled numbers or with different squares or months.

11. Two for the Price of One B

SUGGESTED GRADE SPAN—4 AND UP

This is another good trick to use with a friend, although you can have fun trying it alone, too.

Directions	*Example*

1. Have your friend select any two 2-digit numbers.   24 & 37
2. Multiply either of them by 5 (24).   120
3. Add 36.   156

4. Multiply by 20.	3120
5. Add the second number.	3157
6. Now take the calculator back from your friend, without showing him/her what you are doing, and subtract 720.	2437

Now you can tell your friend his/her first and second numbers. Try it with several different numbers.

Brain-stretcher! Can you show why it works?

12. Three for the Price of One
SUGGESTED GRADE
SPAN—4 AND UP

This is a trick similar to #11.

Directions	*Example*
1. Have your friend select any three 1-digit numbers.	3, 7, 9
2. Multiply the first by 2.	6
3. Add 5.	11
4. Multiply by 5.	55
5. Add the second number.	62
6. Multiply by 10.	620
7. Add the third number.	629
8. Subtract 250.	379

The result should always give the original three numbers in order. You can do a variation with this by having your friend pick a 3-digit number originally. Then change the directions to "Multiply the *100's* digit by 2," etc.

Brain-stretcher! Can you show why this works?

13. Two for the Price of One C

Directions	*Example*
1. Again have your friend select two 2-digit numbers.	24, 59
2. Enter one of the numbers.	59
3. Add the value of the next greater.	119
	(59 + 60)
4. Multiply by 5.	595
5. Multiply by 10.	5950
6. Add 72.	6022
7. Add the second original number.	6046
8. Subtract 122.	5924

The result should always give the original two numbers in the order in which they were used in the problem. Try it with several pairs. As with #12, you can have your friend begin by selecting a 4-digit number, then "breaking it" into two 2-digit numbers.

Brain-stretcher! Can you show why this works?

14. Baffling Birthday B

This is another good trick to use with a friend whose birthday you don't know exactly. Give your friend the calculator to use as you give directions. The example below is for someone whose birthday is May 23 and who is 18 years old. (May = 05.)

Directions	*Example*
1. Enter a 4-digit number so that the first 2 digits are the day of birth and the last two are the month number.	2305
2. Multiply by 2.	4610
3. Add 5.	4615

4. Multiply by 10.   46150
5. Multiply by 5.   230750
6. Add your age, then press the
   "equals" button.   230768
7. Now take the calculator back from
   your friend, and without letting
   him/her see what you are doing,
   subtract 250.   230518

Now tell your friend his/her birthday and age:
Middle two digits (05) are the month (May); first
two, the day (23); last two, the age (18).

Brain-stretcher! Can you show why this works?

15. Don't Flip Your Lid   SUGGESTED GRADE
                                    SPAN—4 AND UP

One of the things people have discovered they can do
with calculators for fun is send "messages." Certain
numerals look very much like certain letters when
the calculator is turned so the display is upside down.
Below are some fun problems with hidden messages
you can try:

a) Can you name the star of a famous "chiller"
   movie? To find the answer, do:
   1. 43×56
   2. Add 300
   3. Multiply by 3
   4. Subtract 46—Flip!

b) A football player collided with another player
   because he did the opposite of what he should
   have done. What did he do?
   1. 57×36
   2. Subtract 198
   3. Divide by 3
   4. Subtract 6—Flip!

c) What did the teenager with the strange accent say was his favorite hobby? To find the answer, do:
1. 2,568 + 7,294
2. × 6
3. − 2,066—Flip!

d) If you're on your toes, you can get a job here! To find out, do:
1. 873 × 98
2. + 19016
3. × 10
4. + 8—Flip!

Brain-stretcher! Make a table of all numerals which, when flipped, resemble letters. Then try to make some message puzzles of your own.

16. Snake Eyes   SUGGESTED GRADE SPAN—7 AND UP

If you and a friend have three dice, here is another trick you can do.

Directions	*Example*
1. Have your friend place the dice with any numbers showing and in an order. (This should be hidden from you.)	2, 5, 6
2. Your friend then enters the 6-digit number formed by the numbers on top of the dice (2, 5, 6) followed by the numbers on the bottoms in the same order (5, 2, 1).	256521
3. Divide by 37.	6933
4. Divide by 3.	2311
5. Then take the calculator back from your friend, and subtract 7.	2304
6. Divide by 9.	256

You can then tell your friend how the dice were set up originally: 2 first, 5 second, and 6 third. You can also tell the original 6-digit number if you remember that the sum of the opposite faces of a die must be 7. Therefore, on the bottom of 2 is 5; 5, 2; 6, 1.

17. Partridge in a Pear Tree

This trick is especially good to use around the holiday season. You may remember some of the song "Partridge in a Pear Tree."

"On the first day of Christmas my true love gave to me
A partridge in a pear tree.
On the second day of Christmas my true love gave to me
Two turtle doves and a partridge in a pear tree."

The question is, what is the *total* number of gifts received during the twelve days? Be careful—this is a tricky one.

18. The Odds Are in Your Favor

In Chapter 2 a trick is explained for finding quickly the sum of all counting numbers up to a chosen even number. The trick below is an even easier way for finding the sum of all *odd* numbers $(1 + 3 + 5 + \ldots)$ up to any designated odd number.

Ask a friend to select any odd number. Warn him not to make it too great for his own sake! (Suggest a number not greater than 59.) Then have your friend add all the odd numbers up to the one picked. Suppose the number picked is 37. Then your friend does

1 + 3 + 5 + . . . + 37 on the calculator, writing the answer, but hiding it from you.

When your friend gives you the calculator:
1. Add 1 to the original greatest odd number used (38).
2. Divide by 2 (19).
3. Multiply that result by itself (361).

You can tell your friend that the sum is 361. (If you have two calculators available, you can do your calculations while your friend is still hard at work adding!)

Brain-stretcher! Can you explain or prove why this works?

19. More Odds in Your Favor

SUGGESTED GRADE
SPAN—7 AND UP

This trick is similar to #18, except this time you can find the sum of all counting numbers up to a designated odd number (1 + 2 + 3 . . .). Again, let your friend select the "top" odd number and begin adding on one calculator. Suppose your friend chooses 43. Meanwhile, you do the following on another calculator:

1. Add 1 to the "top" number (44).
2. Divide by 2 (22).
3. Multiply the result by itself (484).
4. Multiply that by 2 (968).
5. Subtract the result of step 2 from the result of step 4 (946).

That result (946) should be the sum of (1 + 2 + 3 + . . . + 43).

20. Watching Your P's and Q's

SUGGESTED GRADE
SPAN—7 AND UP

Directions	Example
1. Select a 3-digit number between 100 and 200	P: 146
and another anywhere from 201 to 999.	Q: 378
2. Subtract P from 999.	853
3. Add Q.	1231
4. Ignore the thousands in the answer; add 1 to the rest.	232
5. Subtract that number from Q.	146

Do this for several numbers. What always happens?

Brain-stretcher! Can you explain why this always happens?

21. Another Birthday Trick

SUGGESTED GRADE
SPAN—7 AND UP

This is somewhat similar to the other tricks in this chapter dealing with finding birthdays. The directions are:

1. Write the number of the month in which you were born.
2. Add to it the next greater number.
3. Multiply by 50.
4. Add the number of months in a year.
5. Add the day of the month on which the birthday falls.
6. Multiply by 100.
7. Add the number of weeks in a year.
8. Add the number formed by the last two digits of the year in which you were born.
9. Subtract 6252.

If you did this correctly, the first digit or first two digits give the number of the month; the next two, the day number; the last two, the last two digits of the year.

22. Spring Fun SUGGESTED GRADE SPAN—7 AND UP

This trick is particularly good to do on March 31. The directions are:

1. Write any 3-digit number with different first and last digits.
2. Write the number formed by reversing the digits.
3. Enter the greater of these in your calculator; subtract the other.
4. Add to your result in step #3 the number formed by reversing its digits. (If the answer in step #3 is 99, add 990.)
5. Multiply by 10,000.
6. Subtract 7,333,616. Write that result on paper.
7. Clear. Do 100 − 73. Add those two digits to your number on the paper.
8. Under each 2 in that number write P; each 3, L; each 4, R; each 5, O; each 6, F; each 7, A; and each 8, I.
9. Read your result backward.

23. Special Brain-Stretchers SUGGESTED GRADE SPAN—7 AND UP

You have seen a number of different kinds of tricks in this chapter. You may have been able to do many of the brain-stretcher explanations or proofs. If so, you'll want to try one or more of these:

a) Make up a number trick so that you always end up with the same number you started with.

b) Make up a number trick so that you always end up with some constant value.
c) Make up a puzzle similar to the birthday tricks.

SELECTED ANSWERS

Most of these answers are in the form of simple algebraic proofs. It may help to refer back to the directions to see how the "proof" develops.

1. You always get the 4-digit number with which you started.

2. N
$N + 25$
$2N + 50$
$2N + 46$
$N + 23$
23

3. $10a + b$ or N
$10a + b + 10$ $N + 10$
$20a + 2b + 20$ $2N + 20$
$20a + 2b + 120$ $2N + 120$
$10a + b + 60$ $N + 60$
60 60

4. M
$10M$
$10M + 20$
$100M + 200$
$100M + 365$
$100M + A + 365$
$100M + A$

5.
  a
  5a
  5a + 3
  10a + 6
  10a + b + 6
  10a + b

6.

a	a + 1	a + 2
a + 7	a + 8	a + 9
a + 14	a + 15	a + 16

The sum found by adding these 9 terms is 9a + 72.
The smallest number.   a
Add 8:   a + 8
Multiply by 9:   9a + 72

7.
  10a + b
  20a + 2b
  20a + 2b + 4
  100a + 10b + 20
  100a + 10b + 32
  1000a + 100b + 320
  1000a + 100b
  10a + b

8.
  N
  6N
  6N + 48
  30N + 240
  30N + 300
  N + 10
  10

9.   N
       3N
       3N + 30
       15N + 150
       15N + 750
       N + 50
       N

11.   10a + b
        50a + 5b
        50a + 5b + 36
        1000a + 100b + 720
        1000a + 100b + 10c + d + 720
        1000a + 100b + 10c + d

12.   p
        2p
        2p + 5
        10p + 25
        10p + q + 25
        100p + 10q + 250
        100p + 10q + r + 250
        100p + 10q + r

13.   10a + b and 10c + d
        10a + b
        20a + 2b + 1
        100a + 10b + 5
        1000a + 100b + 50
        1000a + 100b + 122
        1000a + 100b + 10c + d + 122
        1000a + 100b + 10c + d

14.   D + M   D: 10a + b   (date)
        2D + 2M   M: 10c + d   (month)
        2D + 2M + 5   A: 10e + f   (age)

20D + 20M + 50
100D + 100M + 250
100D + 100M + A + 250
100D + 100M + A

(1000a + 100b) becomes 100D, but D was originally 2 places further left, making it 100,000a + 10,000b. The same is done for the other places. You can also do a proof with original place values and 6 variables used.

15. a) BLOB
    b) ZIG
    c) GOILS
    d) BOLSHOI

17. 364—one for every other day of the year except Christmas!

18. By adding 1 to the "top" number and dividing by 2, you find the arithmetic average of the numbers. Thus, there will be that number of addends, each of which also has that value, so we multiply it by itself for the total.

20. One key comes in step 4. By "ignoring" the thousands and adding 1 to the remaining 3-digit number, we're really subtracting 999 from the value in step 4. Since we added Q in step 3 and subtracted the original from 999, the result of step 4 plus P is Q. Thus, subtracting it from Q leaves P.

22. APRIL FOOL!

Chapter 2

It All Adds Up

1. Magic 3   SUGGESTED GRADE SPAN—4, 5

	Example
Enter any 3-digit number in your calculator.	588
Add the next lower number.	+ 587
Add the next higher number.	+ 589
	1764
Add the digits of the sum. (1 + 7 + 6 + 4)	18
Add the digits of the new sum (1 + 8)	9

(Continue doing this until you get a 1-digit number.)

What is true of every 1-digit number you get? Try several original 3-digit numbers to see.

2. Across and Down   SUGGESTED GRADE SPAN—4, 5

Look at the two examples below.

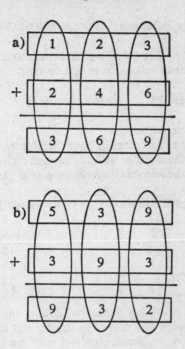

You should notice that the numbers across (addends and sum) read exactly the same as the numbers if read down in both problems.

Find the sum for the two problems below. See if the same pattern occurs as in the examples.

a)   426
    + 258

b)   358
    + 528

To see if the pattern always works, try a problem you make up.

Brain-stretcher! Can you make up a problem that does have the across-and-down pattern of the four above?

3. Playful Palindromes SUGGESTED GRADE SPAN—4-6

A *palindrome* is a number that reads exactly the same from right to left as from left to right.

Examples: 121   26162   3993   487784

Directions
1. Enter any number in your calculator.
2. Add the number with the reverse digits.
3. Add the number with the reverse digits of 2.

<table>
<tr><td colspan="2">3-Digit Example</td><td colspan="2">4-Digit Example</td></tr>
<tr><td></td><td>367</td><td></td><td>8,394</td></tr>
<tr><td>+</td><td>763</td><td>+</td><td>4,938</td></tr>
<tr><td></td><td>1130</td><td></td><td>13,332</td></tr>
<tr><td>+</td><td>0311</td><td>+</td><td>23,331</td></tr>
<tr><td></td><td>1441</td><td></td><td>36,663</td></tr>
</table>

Continue reversing digits and adding until you get a palindrome. (The reversing *usually* works, sooner or later. However, some numbers take many steps.) In the examples you have to reverse twice.

Try to get a palindrome with the numbers below. See how many steps each takes.

a)   237   e)   3,564
b)   789   f) 23,456
c) 4,637   g) 82,193
d) 7,142

Brain-stretcher! Can you find a number that takes at least 6 steps?

4. Watch Your Place   SUGGESTED GRADE SPAN—4–6

Find the sum in the two problems in each set below.
Be careful of the place value!

a)   2 and   2   b)   3 and   3
         13   31   41   14
     + 964   + 469   + 854   + 458

c)   1 and   1   d)   1 and   1
         42   24   43   34
      713   317   821   128
   + 9012 + 2109 + 5134 + 4315

Brain-stretcher! Can you find another combination
starting with a 3-digit number that will work like these
examples? Can you find another starting with a
4-digit number?

5. Addition Whiz Kid   SUGGESTED GRADE SPAN—5, 6

Here is a trick you can use to impress your friends.
Let them do the work on the calculator while you
pretend to do it in your head.

a. Have your friend write four 4-digit numbers on a
   piece of paper.
b. Below these you write four more 4-digit numbers.
   The key is to select your numbers so that the
   digit sum of each number you write, together
   with his, equals 9.

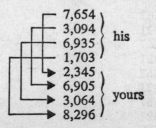

He writes: 7654
You write: 2345, getting
            ———
            9999

c. Have your friend enter all eight numbers on the calculator and find the sum, while you merely write it: 39,996. The sum will always be the same, no matter what numbers your friend chooses.

Brain-stretcher! Can you predict what the sum will always be if you and your friend each write five 4-digit numbers, with you using the same trick? Check your prediction by trying an example on your calculator. If you were right, try some other prediction: six 4-digit numbers; four 5-digit numbers; etc.

6. The Strange Sequence

SUGGESTED GRADE SPAN—6, 7

Find the sums below.

a)   1,234,567
         7,654,321
         1,234,567
     +   7,654,321
     ——————————

b)   1,234,567
         7,654,321
         1,234,567
         7,654,321
         1,234,567
     +   7,654,321
     ——————————

c)   1,234,567
         7,654,321
         1,234,567
         7,654,321
         1,234,567
         7,654,321
         1,234,567
     +   7,654,321
     ——————————

d) What do you think the sum will be if you add 1,234,567 and 7,654,321 to the result of c? Check your guess on the calculator.

Brain-stretcher! Predict the sum if you again add 1,234,567 and 7,654,321 to the result of d. Check your guess.

7. Watch Your Place—B　　　SUGGESTED GRADE
　　　　　　　　　　　　　　　　　SPAN—6, 7

Find the sum of each below.

1	1
21	12
321	123
4321	1234
54321	12345
654321	123456
7654321	1234567
+ 87654321	+ 12345678

8. Staggering Sum　　SUGGESTED GRADE SPAN—6–8

Select five numbers from the table below so that only one number from each row (or column) is selected. (One sample set is circled as a guide.)

17	(22)	23	18	20
(19)	24	25	20	22
12	17	18	13	(15)
15	20	(21)	16	18
27	32	33	(28)	30

Find the sum of the five numbers.

Circle a different set of five, again being certain that
each row and column contains only one.

What do you notice about the two sums? Do you
think this will always work?

Brain-stretcher! Construct a 6 x 6 table for which
the trick works.

9. **Across and Down—B**   SUGGESTED GRADE
                                         SPAN—6–8

Review #2 in this Chapter. Then do the problems
below to see if they fit the same pattern.

a)   11116   b)   24129
        14882   43119
        18325   11327
    + 18202   + 21219

Brain-stretcher! Can you find another set of four
5-digit numbers that works this way?

10. **Addition Whiz Kid—B**   SUGGESTED GRADE
                                         SPAN—7–9

Review #5 in this chapter to see the trick of choosing
your four numbers. Follow a procedure similar to #5,
except allow your friend to choose five numbers,
while you choose only four numbers. Be sure your
four numbers make digit-sums of 9 with four numbers
of his. To get the total sum, subtract 4 from your
friend's number which you did not match. Place a
4 at the beginning of that numeral.

Example:

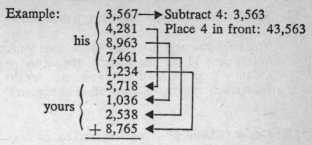

Will this work with numbers of more than 4 digits?

Brain-stretcher! Can you figure out how you would find the sum if your friend wrote only four numbers and you matched only three of them? What if he wrote six and you matched five?

11. Casting Out 9's SUGGESTED GRADE SPAN—7–9

As a rule, the way we check addition for a set of three or more addends is just to add again from bottom to top. Of course, with a calculator we usually assume our first sum is correct and don't check at all. But suppose you pressed the wrong digit by accident . . . or your battery is weak and something went wrong in the circuits? Below is another way to check addition. Look at the example first.

6,489	$(6 + 4 + 8 + 9) = 27$	$(2 + 7) = 9$	
7,536	$(7 + 5 + 3 + 6) = 21$	$(2 + 1) = 3$	$(9 + 3 + 4 + 2)$
8,095	$(8 + 0 + 9 + 5) = 22$	$(2 + 2) = 4$	$= 18$
+3,674	$(3 + 6 + 7 + 4) = 20$	$(2 + 0) = 2$	$(1 + 8) = 9$
25,794	$(2 + 5 + 7 + 9 + 4) = 27$	$(2 + 7) = 9$	Checks!

Make up some column addition problems and check them by casting out nines.

Brain-stretcher! Can you find a shortcut so you don't have to do as many digit sum additions?

12. The "Lulu" Lottery   SUGGESTED GRADE SPAN—7–9

You have just won first prize in the state lottery. The
lottery pays $1 the first year, $2 the second year, $4
the third year, $8 the fourth year, etc., for 20 years.
How much money will you collect altogether?

13. Gauss' "Gimmick"   SUGGESTED GRADE SPAN—7–9

Find the sum of the first 100 counting (natural)
numbers on your calculator: $1 + 2 + 3 + \ldots + 100$.

Gauss, generally regarded as one of the top three
mathematicians of all time, found a short way to do
this problem in his head. The story is told that this
problem was actually given to his class one day. He
startled the instructor by writing the sum almost
immediately. His career as a mathematician was
launched that day. Below is his "gimmick":

$$
\begin{array}{r}
1 + 2 + 3 + \ldots + 50 \\
+\, 100 + 99 + 98 + \ldots + 51 \\
\hline
101 + 101 + 101 + \ldots + 101
\end{array}
$$

Notice that by pairing the numbers as he did, he got
pairs for which the sum would always be 101. There
would be 50 such pairs. Therefore, the sum could
be found by multiplying 101 × 50, or 5,050.

(Gauss, of course, knew the tricks for multiplying by
either of these special numbers without using paper
and pencil. Chapter 4 will discuss some of these
mental multiplication tricks.)

Brain-stretcher! Find the sum of the first 200 counting numbers by using a process similar to Gauss'
"gimmick." Check your answer on your calculator.

14. Fibonacci Follies

Write the first ten numbers of a Fibonacci sequence pattern. That is, select two random numbers for the first and second in your sequence. The third number must be the sum of these first two; the fourth, the sum of the second and third; the fifth, the sum of the third and fourth; etc.

Find the series sum.

Now multiply the seventh number by 11. What do you observe? Check another series to see if it happens again.

If you practice this (and especially if you can learn to multiply by 11 in your head!), you can work this on a friend as another type of "Whiz Kid" problem.

15. Special Brain-Stretchers

a) Find a formula for Gauss' "Gimmick" (#13) for the sum of the first N counting numbers for any even value of N. Check your formula for the value 64.

b) Review the "trick" in #1 of this chapter. Try to prove why it works.

SELECTED ANSWERS

1. It will always be a multiple of 3 (either 3, 6, or 9).

2. The pattern works for both problems. There are many more sets of two 3-digit numbers which work, but it

may take a lot of calculator trials to get another one on your own!

3. Some numbers which take 6 or more reversals to get a palindrome are: 2089 (6 reversals); 672 (8 reversals).
   Note: If you tried 196 or 879, you had a real problem. You can't get a palindrome with these.

4. The sum is the same for the two sets in each of the four examples. Like #2, there are many possible solutions to the brain-stretchers, but it may take many trials to find them.

5. If you and your friend each write five 4-digit numbers with the pattern described, the sum should be 49,995. For six 4-digit numbers it will be 59,994. For four 5-digit numbers it will be 399,996. You are reminded that these mean six sets, four sets, etc., or a total of 12 addends, 8 addends, etc.

6. You can find the actual answers by simple addition. The trick is to find the pattern in the sums. The first digit increases by 1. The repeating digits decrease by 1. The 1's digit decreases by 2, and when you get to the last prediction, you have to decrease by regrouping.

7. The sum is the same for both: 96,021,948.

8. The sum will always be the same; in this case, 105. To get a 6 x 6 table that works, add a row along the

bottom of the given table containing 29, 34, 35, 30 and 32. Add a column along the right containing 21, 23, 16, 19, 31 and 33. (The 33 will be to the right of the 32 you added along the bottom.)

9. As with #2, there are many possible answers.

10. If your friend wrote four and you matched three, subtract 3 from his "extra" number and place a 3 in front of the numeral. If he wrote six and you matched five, subtract 5 from his "extra" and write 5 in front of the numeral.

11. The shortcut is to cast out sets of digits whose sum is 9, or a multiple of 9, prior to finding digit sums. An example is shown below:

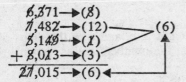

12. $1,048,575

13. Set up the problem this way:

$$
\begin{array}{r}
1 + 2 + 3 + \ldots + 100 \\
+ 200 + 199 + 198 + \ldots + 101 \\
\hline
201 + 201 + 201 + \ldots + 201
\end{array}
$$

You will have 100 sets of 201, so the sum is: 20,100.

14. The sum should always be 11 × seventh number. Two samples are shown below:

#1:	23	58
#2:	47	39
#3:	70	97
#4:	117	136
#5:	187	233
#6:	304	369
#7:	491	602
#8:	795	971
#9:	1286	1573
#10:	2081	2544
Sum:	5401	6622

$$11 \times 491 = 5401 \qquad 6622 = 11 \times 602$$

15. a) The formula is: $\dfrac{N(N+1)}{2}$ (The sum for 1–64 is 2,080.)

b) The proof is: Let a, b, and c be the digits of the original. Then the numbers are as shown below:

$$
\begin{array}{l}
100a + 10b + c \\
100a + 10b + (c - 1) \\
\underline{+\ 100a + 10b + (c + 1)} \\
300a + 30b + 3c \ = \ 3(100a + 10b + c)
\end{array}
$$

Since 3 is a factor here, regardless of the values of a, b and c, the number is always divisible by 3. We can further note that the original sum is always 3 times the value of the first number.

Chapter 3

Take It Away

1. Tricky Triangle

SUGGESTED GRADE SPAN—4, 5

In the triangle below the sum of the numbers in the four circles along each side is to be 100. Fill in the missing numbers to make this work, using all the nine numbers from 21 to 29 once each.

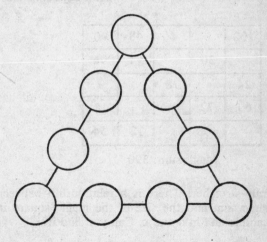

2. Magic Squares

SUGGESTED GRADE SPAN—4, 5

In a *magic square* the sum of every column and row and the two main diagonals is always the same. That number is called the *magic sum*.

This is a magic square.
Its magic sum is 36. Check it.

15	8	13
10	12	14
11	16	9

Complete the magic squares below:

a)

	8	
24		
32		16

Magic sum: 120

b)

	4	6	
10		20	
18	14		24
	28		2

Magic sum: 68

c)

102		6	48	90
	30		84	96
24		78		
60	72			18
	108		12	54

Magic sum: 390

Brain-stretcher! There is a relationship between the magic sum and the size of the magic square in the example and in a and c. Can you find it?

3. Subtraction "Whiz Kid"   SUGGESTED GRADE
                                       SPAN—4, 5

Here is a trick which uses addition and subtraction. You can use it to fool your friends.

Directions	*Example*
1. Have your friend write a 3-digit number with the first and last digits different.	428
2. Then he writes the number he gets by switching the first and last digits.	824
3. He then subtracts the less from the greater on the calculator.	824 − 428
4. Finally, he adds to that result the number formed by reversing its digits.	396 + 693 1,089

(Tell him you already know the answer. It will always be 1,089!)

4. Subtraction "Whiz Kid" B   SUGGESTED GRADE

                                            SPAN—4, 5

This is a lot like #3 above. Stop your friend after he does the subtraction in step 3. Have him tell you the first digit of his answer. You tell him the whole answer.

Here's how! The middle digit is always 9. The sum of the first and last digits is always 9. So if he tells you the first digit is 6, you know the third digit is 3 (6 + 3 = 9) and the number is 693. Notice that this worked in #3.

If he gives you a 7, what is his difference?

5. Don't Flip Your Lid B   SUGGESTED GRADE

                                            SPAN—4 AND UP

In Chapter 1 there were some fun word puzzles which could also be solved by doing problems on the calculator, then flipping it to read the numerals as letters. Below are some more puzzles like those. *Each of these puzzles consists of two-word answers, so read your results carefully when you flip.*

a) What did the bat say when the owl told him to get glasses?
b) What is the secret of success in the stock market?
c) What does a shy boy do when his secret crush smiles at him?
d) What does the harried homemaker call the sound made by the mailman on the first of the month?

If you want to check your answers or find the correct answer to the riddles above, do these problems and flip:

a) $5,000 - 1,649$
b) $18,946,358 + 27,201,377$
c) $7,000,000 - 1,538,466$
d) $23,456,789 + 53,930, 929$

6. Mini-Max   SUGGESTED GRADE SPAN—5–7

Directions	Example
1. Select any 4 digits, not all the same.	3,2,4,1
2. In your calculator enter the greatest 4-digit number (Max) they form.	4,321 (Max)
3. Subtract the least 4-digit number (Min) they form.	$\underline{- 1,234}$ (Min) 3,087
4. Clear your calculator. Enter the Max of that number.	8,730 (Max)
5. Subtract the Min.	$\underline{- 0,378}$ (Min) 8,352
6. Continue this until you get 6,174.	8,532 (Max) $\underline{- 2,358}$ (Min) 6,174

Some numbers, of course, take many more subtractions than others to get 6,174. See how many times you have to do it for the following:
a) 7,1,3,5   b) 2,1,9,8   c) 8,9,9,1

Brain-stretcher! Do it for the digits 2,7,6,3.

7. Subtraction by Addition
SUGGESTED GRADE
SPAN—5–7

The complement of a number (in base 10) is the number which must be added to it to get a sum containing 1 as the first digit and all other digits of 0. That is, the sum of a number and its complement will be 10; 100; 1,000; etc., depending on the number of digits it has. We will work with three-digit numbers in this example.

Example: 527 (original number)
            473 (complement)

To get the complement quickly make the sum in the 1's place 10 (7 + 3) and 9 in the other two places (2 + 7 and 5 + 4).

Now you'll see a technique for subtraction by adding the complement.

Example: 648
          − 259

1. Enter the original number in your
    calculator.   648
2. Add the complement (741) of the
    second (259).   741
                                             ────
                                             1389
3. Cross out the first digit of this sum
    and note your answer.   389
4. Now do the original subtraction problem.

If you did it correctly, you should get the same result (389). Try this with several other problems to see if it always works.

8. Magic Cubes   SUGGESTED GRADE SPAN—6, 7

A magic cube is somewhat like a magic square. The sum of the four numbers at the vertices of each of the six faces must be the same. An example of a magic cube is shown below, with the magic sum = 482.

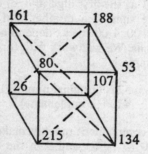

Face Sums
Top: $161 + 188 + 80 + 53 = 482$
Bottom: $26 + 107 + 215 + 134 = 482$
Front: $80 + 53 + 215 + 134 = 482$
Back: $161 + 188 + 26 + 107 = 482$
Left: $161 + 80 + 26 + 215 = 482$
Right: $188 + 53 + 107 + 134 = 482$

Diagonal Plane Sums
Left: $161 + 80 + 107 + 134 = 482$
Right: $188 + 53 + 26 + 215 = 482$

(Note that in a magic cube the sum of the four points of the two diagonal planes is also the same, just as the diagonals are in a magic square.)

Below is a magic cube with some numbers missing. Find them.

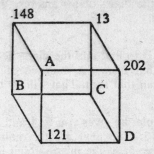

Magic sum: 430

9. Subtraction "Whiz Kid" C

This is a variation of trick #3 of this chapter. Select and write down any 5-digit number with different first and last digits. Write the 5-digit number formed by switching the first and last digits. Subtract the lesser from the greater of these two. Then reverse the digits of that difference and add the new number to the difference, first predicting your answer. Try several other problems to see if the answer is always the same.

Brain-stretcher! In problems of 5 digits, when the difference is 9,999, what number do you have to add? Predict the constant sum if you use 4 digits; if you use 6 digits.

10. Subtraction "Whiz Kid" D

Have a friend enter a 4-digit number in his calculator. Tell him to subtract from it any other 4-digit number containing the same digits. Remind him to be careful that the result isn't negative. Then have him tell you any 3 of the digits of his answer. You then tell him the fourth.

The trick is to first add the digits he gives you. Then subtract that from the multiple of 9 which is next greater than that sum. That will be the missing digit.

For example, he gives you 6, 4 and 3. Adding these, you get 13. The next greater multiple of 9 is 18. $18 - 13 = 5$, so the missing digit is 5.

Practice this until you can do it very quickly.

Brain-stretcher! Will this work for more than 4 digits? Try it for several 5- and 6-digit numbers.

11. Casting Out 9's   SUGGESTED GRADE SPAN—7–9

You may want to review #11 in Chapter 2 on casting out nines in addition.

Look at the example below for the similar process for checking subtraction.

```
   7,438        (22)
 - 2,865      - (21)   = ①
 ─────────     ─────     ①
   4,573        (10)            Checks!
```

Practice checking subtractions by casting out nines with several examples.

12. Accent the Negative

SUGGESTED GRADE
SPAN—8, 9

This is a variation on #8 of this chapter. In these tricks you always subtracted the less from the greater to be sure to avoid negative numbers. Do several in which everything else is the same as #8 except subtract the greater from the less. Do you think the answer will be different than 109,989?

13. Special Brain-Stretcher

SUGGESTED GRADE
SPAN—9 AND UP

Prove why you will always get 1,089 in trick #3 in this chapter.

SELECTED ANSWERS

1.

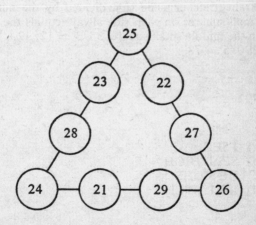

(Your answer may be "mixed" around so that your left side is like the bottom here, or something like that.)

2. a)

64	8	48
24	40	56
32	72	16

b)

32	4	6	26
10	22	20	16
18	14	12	24
8	28	30	2

c)

102	144	6	48	90
138	30	42	84	96
24	36	78	120	132
60	72	114	126	18
66	108	150	12	54

Brain-stretcher: The sum divided by the number of small squares on each side always equals the number in the middle small square. 36/3 = 12; 120/3 = 40; 390/5 = 78

4. 792

5. a) I SEE
b) SELL HIGH
c) HE SIGHS
d) BILL BELL

6. a) one reversal   b) two reversals   c) three reversals

Brain-stretcher: five reversals

7. The number you get by crossing out the first digit of the sum of the original minuend and the complement of the original subtrahend is the same as the difference in the original problem.

8. A = 67   B = 94   C = 175   D = 40

9. For 5-digit numbers the final result is 109,989.

   If the subtraction step (with 5-digit numbers) gives 9,999, add 99,990. This is because 9,999 contains only 4 digits, so we consider its ten-thousands place as 0.

   The sum using 4-digit numbers is 10,989; 6-digit, 1,099,989.

10. Yes, it works for any number of digits if you're given all but one of them.

12. Sample Problem:

	62,519
—	92,516
—	29,997
+	79,992
	49,995

Pattern Chart

1	89,991
2	69,993
3	49,995
4	29,997
5	09,999
6	— 09,999
7	— 29,997
8	— 49,995
9	— 69,993

   The 1–9 in the Pattern Chart represents the difference between the first and last digits in the two numbers

subtracted. Note also the pattern of first and last digits in the final results.

13. Let a, b and c represent the digits of the original number (a $\neq$ c).

$$\begin{array}{r} 100a + 10b + c \\ - (100c + 10b + a) \\ \hline 99a - 99c = 99(a-c) \end{array}$$

Since a and c represent 1-digit values and a $\neq$ c, it is evident that the possible values of a–c can only be 1–9. Thus, the differences can only be 99 times each value 1–9, or: 99, 198, 297, 396, 495, 594, 693, 792, 891.

Therefore, the only numbers added to these are, respectively, 990, 891, etc.

$$\begin{array}{ccccc} 099 & 198 & 297 & 396 & 495 \\ +990 & +891 & +792 & +693 & +594 \\ \hline 1,089 & 1,089 & 1,089 & 1,089 & 1,089 \end{array}$$

The rest of the added pairs are merely the inversions of these.

Chapter 4

Multiplication Magic

1. The Magic of 9's   SUGGESTED GRADE SPAN—4, 5

Do the first three problems on paper or with your calculator. Then try to guess the rest of the answers before multiplying. Check your guesses.

$$99 \times 12 =$$
$$99 \times 23 =$$
$$99 \times 34 =$$
$$99 \times 45 =$$
$$99 \times 56 =$$
$$99 \times 67 =$$
$$99 \times 78 =$$
$$99 \times 89 =$$

Now do this table.

$$100 \times 12 - 12 =$$
$$100 \times 23 - 23 =$$
$$100 \times 34 - 34 =$$
$$100 \times 45 - 45 =$$
$$100 \times 56 - 56 =$$
$$100 \times 67 - 67 =$$
$$100 \times 78 - 78 =$$
$$100 \times 89 - 89 =$$

Brain-stretcher! Can you describe a way to multiply numbers by 99 in your head?

2. The Surprising Switch

Do each pair of multiplication problems below.

a)   39   and   93   b)   84   and   48
    $\times$ 62 $\times$ 26 $\times$ 12 $\times$ 21

c)   26   and   62   d)   63   and   36
    $\times$ 31 $\times$ 13 $\times$ 12 $\times$ 21

Do you think this kind of digit switch will always give the same product? Try it with a problem of your own or

    56   and   65
  $\times$ 24 $\times$ 42

Brain-stretcher! Can you figure out why the first four problems worked? If you think you know, try to make up another problem and check to see if you are right.

3. Eleven Come Eleven   SUGGESTED GRADE SPAN—4, 5

Do the first three problems. Try to predict the rest of the answers. Then check your guesses on the calculator.

$11 \times 11 =$
$11 \times 22 =$
$11 \times 33 =$
$11 \times 44 =$
$11 \times 55 =$
$11 \times 66 =$
$11 \times 77 =$
$11 \times 88 =$
$11 \times 99 =$

Brain-stretcher! Can you figure out a way to multiply by 11 in your head by adding? If you think you know, check it by guessing 11 × 36. Then check your answer by multiplying.

4. Seeing Triple?   SUGGESTED GRADE SPAN—4, 5

Do the first three problems. Try to predict the rest of the answers. Then check your guesses on the calculator.

```
3 7 ×  3 =
3 7 ×  6 =
3 7 ×  9 =
3 7 × 1 2 =
3 7 × 1 5 =
3 7 × 1 8 =
3 7 × 2 1 =
3 7 × 2 4 =
3 7 × 2 7 =
```

5. More Fun with 9's   SUGGESTED GRADE SPAN—4, 5

Do the first three problems. Guess the rest; then check.

```
1 × 9109 =
2 × 9109 =
3 × 9109 =
4 × 9109 =
5 × 9109 =
6 × 9109 =
7 × 9109 =
8 × 9109 =
9 × 9109 =
```

6. Puzzling Pattern   SUGGESTED GRADE SPAN—5, 6

Do the six problems below.

$1 \times 142{,}857 =$
$2 \times 142{,}857 =$
$3 \times 142{,}857 =$
$4 \times 142{,}857 =$
$5 \times 142{,}857 =$
$6 \times 142{,}857 =$

What do you notice about the digits in each product?
Do you think there is a pattern here? Try $7 \times 142{,}857$ to see.

7. More Magic of 9's   SUGGESTED GRADE SPAN—5, 6

Do the first three problems below. Try to predict the rest; check.

$999 \times 12 =$
$999 \times 23 =$
$999 \times 34 =$
$999 \times 45 =$
$999 \times 56 =$
$999 \times 67 =$
$999 \times 78 =$
$999 \times 89 =$

Now do this table.

$1000 \times 12 - 12 =$
$1000 \times 23 - 23 =$
$1000 \times 34 - 34 =$
$1000 \times 45 - 45 =$
$1000 \times 56 - 56 =$
$1000 \times 67 - 67 =$
$1000 \times 78 - 78 =$
$1000 \times 89 - 89 =$

Brain-stretcher! Can you describe a way to multiply numbers by 999 in your head?

8. Everything's Coming Up
SUGGESTED GRADE SPAN—5, 6

Do the six problems below.

$483 \times 12 =$
$154 \times 48 =$
$186 \times 39 =$
$198 \times 27 =$
$297 \times 18 =$
$138 \times 42 =$

Look carefully at the digits of each problem and the digits of its product. What do you notice? Do you think this always works?

9. A Trick from Seeing Triple
SUGGESTED GRADE SPAN—5, 6

Ask a friend to pick a 3-digit number with all digits the same (like 777). Have him tell you only the sum of the digits, but not his number. You can use the chart in #4 to tell him his number, or you can multiply his sum by 37.

Brain-stretcher! Is there a shortcut you can use so you don't need either the chart or multiplying by 37?

10. The Surprising Switch B
SUGGESTED GRADE SPAN—5–7

Do each pair of multiplication problems below.

a) 602 and 206   b) 408 and 804
    $\times 103$ $\times 301$ $\times 201$ $\times 102$

c) 936 and 639   d) 431 and 134
    $\times 213$ $\times 312$ $\times 268$ $\times 862$

Do you think this kind of digit switch will always give the same product? Try it with a problem of your own or

$$563 \text{ and } 365$$
$$\underline{\times 248} \quad \underline{\times 842}$$

Brain-stretcher! Can you figure out why the first four problems worked? If you think you know, try to make up another problem and check to see if you are right.

11. All and Nothing   SUGGESTED GRADE SPAN—6, 7

Do the three problems below.

a) 101 b) 101 c) 101
   $\underline{\times 34}$ $\underline{\times 72}$ $\underline{\times 59}$

Now predict 101 × 85. Check your prediction.

Do the three problems below.

a) 10101 b) 10101 c) 10101
   $\underline{\times 34}$ $\underline{\times 72}$ $\underline{\times 59}$

Now predict 10101 × 85. Check your prediction.

Do the three problems below.

a) 1001 b) 1001 c) 1001
   $\underline{\times 345}$ $\underline{\times 724}$ $\underline{\times 598}$

Now predict 1001 × 854. Check your prediction.

Brain-stretchers! Can you describe a shortcut for multiplying by 101 in your head? What about 1001?

12. 1089 Revisited SUGGESTED GRADE SPAN—6, 7

Do the first two problems in your head or with your calculator. Then try to predict the rest before you multiply. Check your predictions.

$9 \times 1089 =$
$9 \times 10989 =$
$9 \times 109989 =$
$9 \times 1099989 =$
$9 \times 10999989 =$

Do the same thing with this group.

$4 \times 2178 =$
$4 \times 21978 =$
$4 \times 219978 =$
$4 \times 2199978 =$
$4 \times 21999978 =$

13. Seeing Triple Double? SUGGESTED GRADE SPAN—6, 7

Do the first three problems. Predict the rest; then check.

$15,873 \times 7 =$
$15,873 \times 14 =$
$15,873 \times 21 =$
$15,873 \times 28 =$
$15,873 \times 35 =$
$15,873 \times 42 =$
$15,873 \times 49 =$
$15,873 \times 56 =$
$15,873 \times 63 =$

14. Eighter from Decatur SUGGESTED GRADE SPAN—6, 7

Do the first three problems. Predict the rest; then check.

$$9 \times 9 + 7 =$$
$$9 \times 98 + 6 =$$
$$9 \times 987 + 5 =$$
$$9 \times 9876 + 4 =$$
$$9 \times 98765 + 3 =$$
$$9 \times 987654 + 2 =$$
$$9 \times 9876543 + 1 =$$

Although the answer won't fit on your calculator, can you guess what $9 \times 98765432 + 0 = ?$

You can check your guess by using paper and pencil, or you can do $9 \times 8765432 + 810,000,000$. (The last is from the 9×9 million, which is the only part not included in the first product.)

Brain-stretcher! Can you write the form that the next step would be if you continued the same pattern in writing the problems? Also, can you predict the answer?

15. More Fun with 37's SUGGESTED GRADE SPAN—6, 7

Do the first three problems. Predict the rest; then check.

$$37037 \times 3 =$$
$$37037 \times 6 =$$
$$37037 \times 9 =$$
$$37037 \times 12 =$$
$$37037 \times 15 =$$
$$37037 \times 18 =$$
$$37037 \times 21 =$$
$$37037 \times 24 =$$
$$37037 \times 27 =$$

16. Seeing Triple Double Again?   SUGGESTED GRADE
SPAN—6, 7

$3367 \times 33 =$
$3367 \times 66 =$
$3367 \times 99 =$
$3367 \times 132 =$
$3367 \times 165 =$
$3367 \times 198 =$
$3367 \times 231 =$
$3367 \times 264 =$
$3367 \times 297 =$

17. More Magic with 9's B   SUGGESTED GRADE
SPAN—6, 7

Do the first three problems. Predict the rest; then
check.

$2222222 \times 9 =$
$3333333 \times 9 =$
$4444444 \times 9 =$
$5555555 \times 9 =$
$6666666 \times 9 =$
$7777777 \times 9 =$
$8888888 \times 9 =$
$9999999 \times 9 =$

18. More Magic with 8's   SUGGESTED GRADE SPAN—6, 7

Do the first three problems. Predict the rest; then
check.

$9 \times 1 - 1 =$
$9 \times 21 - 1 =$
$9 \times 321 - 1 =$
$9 \times 4321 - 1 =$
$9 \times 54321 - 1 =$
$9 \times 654321 - 1 =$
$9 \times 7654321 - 1 =$

Although the answer won't fit on your calculator, can you guess what $9 \times 87654321 - 1 = ?$

Check your prediction.

Brain-stretcher! Write what the next problem would be, together with the answer.

19. Guess the Missing Number

You may want to review #11 in this chapter.

Tell a friend to pick any 3-digit number and multiply it by 1001 on the calculator. Ask him for the first three digits in his answer; you can then tell him the sum of the digits in his number. Just add the digits he gives you and double.

20. "Mummy" Multiplication

The Egyptians had an unusual way of doing multiplication. Look at the explanation and example below.

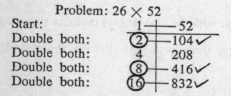

Problem: 26×52

Start:	1 — 52
Double both:	②— 104 ✓
Double both:	4 — 208
Double both:	⑧— 416 ✓
Double both:	⑯— 832 ✓

In the column with the 1 circle numbers which add to 26, the other factor.

Add the numbers beside them in the other column. $832 + 416 + 104 = 1352$

Do the problem 29 × 47 by this method.

If the smaller factor was much greater than 50, the Egyptians used a shortcut by working with multiples of 10. Look at the explanation and example below.

Problem: 73 × 84

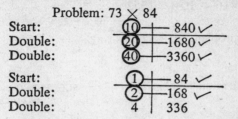

Start:	⑩	840 ✓
Double:	⑳	1680 ✓
Double:	㊵	3360 ✓
Start:	①	84 ✓
Double:	②	168 ✓
Double:	4	336

In the column with the 10 circle numbers which add to 70, the tens' part of the other factor. In the column with the 1, circle numbers which add to 3, the 1's part of the other factor.

Add all the numbers beside each circled number in the other column.

3360 + 1680 + 840 + 168 + 84 = 6132

Do the problem 95 × 89 this way.

Brain-stretcher! Do the problem 158 × 243 this way.

21. The Doubling-Halving Method SUGGESTED GRADE
SPAN—7, 8

There is another ancient multiplying technique. Look at the example and explanation below.

Problem: 26 × 52

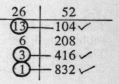

Start:	26	52
Halve left; double right	⑬	104 ✓
Halve left; double right*	6	208
Halve left; double right	③	416 ✓
Halve left; double right*	①	832 ✓
Stop at 1 in left.		

* Disregard remainder.

Circle all odd numbers on the left (including start). Add all the numbers beside the circled numbers on the right.

$$832 + 416 + 104 = 1352$$

Do the problem 35×76 this way.

22. Multiplication "Whiz Kid"
SUGGESTED GRADE
SPAN—7–9

Here is another of those tricks you can use to dazzle your friend. Read the explanation and example below.

Directions	*Example*
1. Have your friend enter any 3-digit number on his/her calculator and tell you what it is.	689
2. Have him/her select a second 3-digit number.	473
3. Have him/her find their product and record it, but not tell you.	325,897
4. Now have your friend multiply his/her first number (689) by the 3-digit number whose digit sum with 473 is 999 (526).	362,414
5. Finally, have him/her add the two products, while you give him/her the answer.	688,311

The trick is to get the first 3 digits of the answer by subtracting 1 from his first number (689 − 1 = 688). The final 3 digits are those which form a digit sum of 999 with the first 3 digits (*311* + 688 = 999).

Brain-stretcher! Can you explain why this works?

23. **Multiplication without Multiplying** SUGGESTED GRADE
SPAN—7–9

Suppose the multiplication key on your calculator isn't working. You can still do multiplication problems by adding, if you are careful. Below is an example of how you would do 8,756 × 234 on your calculator without using the "×" key:

Step 1:   875600 (100 × 8756)
Step 2: + 875600 (100 × 8756) } (200 × 8756)
              1751200
Step 3: + 87560 (10 × 8756)
              1838760
Step 4: + 87560 (10 × 8756) } (30 × 8756)
              1926320
Step 5: + 87560 (10 × 8756)
              2013880
Step 6: +   8756 (1 × 8756)
              2022636
Step 7: +   8756 (1 × 8756)
              2031392
Step 8: +   8756 (1 × 8756) } (4 × 8756)
              2040148
Step 9: +   8756 (1 × 8756)
              2048904   8,756 × 234 = 2,048,904

You don't have to do much writing. Just keep a tally each time you add a multiple with the correct number of 0's until you've added the correct value by digit in each place. A little chart like the one below works:

H   T   0
//   ///   ////

Note: The process above is what computers do to multiply. They perform successive addition until reaching the product. (Of course, they do it much faster!) The next chapter will show how you can (and computers do) divide by repeated subtraction.

Try to do some multiplication problems this way.

24. Casting Out 9's   SUGGESTED GRADE SPAN—7–9

You may want to review #11 in Chapter 2. Also, look at the example below to see an illustration of casting out nines to check multiplication.

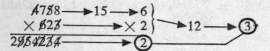

Does not check! Find the error.

Check some multiplication problems this way.

25. Special Brain-Stretchers!   SUGGESTED GRADE SPAN—9 AND UP

a) Review #2 in this chapter. Try to prove that the trick works.
b) Review #10 in this chapter. Even if you didn't discover the rule when you first tried it, see if you can use algebra to discover what the relationships must be.

SELECTED ANSWERS

1. Add two zeroes (multiply by 100) to the other number (multiplicand); then subtract that number (multiplicand) from the result.

2. The product of the tens' digits must equal the product of the ones' digits. For example, $3 \times 6 = 9 \times 2$, so $39 \times 62 = 93 \times 26$.

3. Shift the digits one place to the left of the original (multiply by 10) and add it to the original (multiply by 1). For example, to do 11×36, add:

$$\begin{array}{r} 36 \\ +\ \ 36 \\ \hline 396 \end{array}$$

6. All of the digits in 142,857 appear in each product in order, but beginning with a different digit each time. However, it doesn't continue beyond the first six. Notice that $7 \times 142,857 = 999,999$!

7. Add three zeroes (multiply by 1000) to the other number; then subtract that number from the result.

8. Each of the digits 1–9 appears in one of the factors or the product. This only works in special cases.

9. Just divide his sum by 3 and you'll know the digit of his original 3-digit number with all digits the same.

10. You may have guessed that it would work if the product of the hundreds' digits was equal to the product of the ones'. However, if you tried more examples, you would find that that was not enough.

11. 101 shortcut: Add two zeroes to the original (multiply by 100) and add the original to that result.

1001 shortcut: Add three zeroes to the original (multiply by 1000) and add the original to that result.

14. $9 \times 98765432 + 0 = 888888888$
$9 \times 987654321 - 1 = 8888888888$

18. $9 \times 87654321 - 1 = 788888888$
$9 \times 987654321 - 1 = 8888888888$

20.

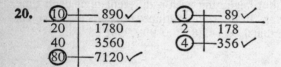

$$7120 + 890 + 356 + 89 = 8455$$

$$24300 + 9720 + 2430 + 1944 = 38,394$$

21.

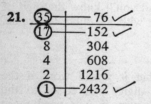

$$2432 + 152 + 76 = 2660$$

22. It is similar to multiplying by 999 in your head.

25. a) *first product:* $(10a + b)(10c + d) = 100ac + 10(bc + ad) + bd$
second product: $(10b + a)(10d + c) = 100bd + 10(bc + ad) + ac$
Note that the tens' digit is the same in both products; the hundreds' and ones' digits have switched places.

b) *first product:* $(100a + 10b + c)(100d + 10e + f) = 10,000ad + 1,000(ae + bd) + 100(af + be + cd) + 10(bf + ce) + cf$
second product: $(100c + 10b + a)(100f + 10e + d) = 10,000cf + 1,000(ce + bf) + 100(af + be + cd) + 10(bd + ae) + ad$
Comparing these, we note that the hundreds' digit is the same in both. However, for the first and last digits to switch, ad must equal cf. But, in addition, for the second and fourth to switch, $ae + bd$ must equal $ce + bf$. Thus, for the trick to work, all three conditions must be met.

Chapter 5

Divide and Conquer

1. Divisibility by 3   SUGGESTED GRADE SPAN—4, 5

Reminder: The digit sum of a number is found by adding each of its digits. The digit sum of 368,249 = 3 + 6 + 8 + 2 + 4 + 9 = 32.

To see if a number is divisible by 3 by using your calculator, divide it by 3 and see whether the answer is a whole number. If there is a decimal in the answer, the number is not divisible by 3.

Do the problems shown in the chart below. One example is done for you.

Number	Divisible by 3?	Digit Sum	Divisible by 3?
159	Yes	15	Yes
268			
792			
1641			
27894			

Based on this, what seems to be true about when a number is divisible by 3? Check your theory by deciding if the following numbers are divisible by 3 first, then dividing to check.

a) 3,695   b) 7,461   c) 38,592

2. Divisibility by 9   SUGGESTED GRADE SPAN—4, 5

Do the problems on the chart below. One example is done for you.

Number	Divisible by 9?	Digit Sum	Divisible by 9?
159	No	15	No
268			
792			
1641			
27894			

Based on this chart, what seems to be true about when a number is divisible by 9? Check your theory by deciding if the following numbers are divisible by 9 first, then dividing to check.

a) 3,496   b) 7,461   c) 38,592

Brain-stretcher! Is every number that is divisible by 3 also divisible by 9? Is every number that is divisible by 9 also divisible by 3? If you said "Yes" to either question, why do you think it is so?

3. 99 Revisited   SUGGESTED GRADE SPAN—4, 5

We've seen in earlier chapters that 99 is a special number. Here is a special thing about 99 and division you can check.

	Directions	*Example*
1.	Pick any 3-digit number so that not all digits are the same.	589
2.	Write the reverse number.	985
3.	Subtract the lesser from the greater.	396
4.	Divide by 99.	4

Is every answer you get for step 3 divisible by 99?

You can also do this as a trick with a friend. Have him tell you the first digit in his answer after he subtracts. You then can tell him what he will get when he divides by 99. If he tells you 1, his quotient will be 2. If he tells you 2, his quotient will be 3. In other words, his quotient will always be 1 greater than the number he tells you as the first digit.

Be careful about one thing in this trick. If your friend tells you his first digit is 9, that means his difference is only 99. Then his quotient is 1. This is different from the rule given above.

4. Amazing Tautonyms

SUGGESTED GRADE
SPAN—4–6

A number tautonym is a numeral which contains a sequence of digits repeated once. Examples are: 66 (6 repeats once); 1212 (12 repeats once); 234234 (234 repeats once); and 59835983 (5983 repeats once).

Directions	Example
1. Select any 3-digit numeral.	287
2. Enter its tautonym in your calculator.	287287
3. Divide by 13.	22099
4. Divide by 11.	2009
5. Divide by 7.	287

Do this for several numbers. What always happens?

Brain-stretcher! Can you explain why the same thing always happens?

5. Divisibility by 4   SUGGESTED GRADE SPAN—5, 6

Do the problems on the chart below. One example is done for you.

Number	Divisible by 4?	Last 2 Digits	Divisible by 4?
648	Yes	48	Yes
1235			
2572			
36718			
48144			

Based on the results of the chart, what seems to be true about when a number is divisible by 4? Check your theory by first predicting whether the numbers below are divisible by 4, then checking with your calculator.

a) 7824   b) 67826   c) 89936

Brain-stretcher! How does this rule for divisibility by 4 relate to the rule for divisibility by 2? Based on that, what do you think the rule for divisibility by 8 will be? (Do not look at the answer for this second question before you try the next page.)

6. Divisibility by 8   SUGGESTED GRADE SPAN—5, 6

Do the problems on the chart below. One example is done for you.

Number	Divisible by 8?	Last 3 Digits	Divisible by 8?
1824	Yes	824	Yes
24616			
38294			
98768			
12456			

Based on the results of the chart, what seems to be true about when a number is divisible by 8? Check your theory by first predicting whether the numbers below are divisible by 8, then checking with your calculator.

a) 12,328   b) 23,912   c) 794,314

7. Sneaky Seven   SUGGESTED GRADE SPAN—5, 6

	Directions	*Example*
1.	Select any 3-digit number which is *not* divisible by 7. (You can check your selection with your calculator.)	748
2.	Enter its tautonym in your calculator. (See #4, this chapter.)	748748
3.	Now divide to see if that number is divisible by 7.	106964

Try this for several different original 3-digit numbers. Be sure to start with one which is *not* divisible by 7.

Brain-stretcher! Why will the tautonym always be divisible by 7 even though the original number is not?

8. Don't Flip Your Lid C

Below are four more word puzzles similar to #5 in
Chapter 3. First try to solve the riddle. To check your
answer do the problem and flip to read the answer.
The number of words in a–c is two; part d is a three-
word answer. C and d also require an additional step.

a) Ed Sullivan used to have one on TV every week.
   Wilt Chamberlain has one all the time. What is it?
b) What is a fun-filled party in a hive called?
c) What do they call the musician who hitchhikes to
   all of his concerts?
d) How does the art collector refer to his only paint-
   ing by Da Vinci?

Below are the problems you can use to help find the
answers:

a) $\dfrac{5202 \times 9953}{17}$

b) $\dfrac{1008 \times 80389}{24}$

c) $\dfrac{2432 \times 10583}{32}$

Write the answer you get for this step on paper.
Clear the calculator. Reenter the whole number you
got as a decimal with the point first and another
zero last.

d) $\dfrac{150 \times 74141}{3}$

Write your answer on paper; clear. Reenter the
answer as a decimal with the point first.

9.   Sneakier Seven   SUGGESTED GRADE SPAN—6, 7

	Directions	*Example*
1.	Select any 2-digit number which is *not* divisible by 7.	47
2.	Enter the 6-digit numeral formed by repeating these digits 3 times.	474747
3.	Now divide to see if that number is divisible by 7.	67821

Try this for several different original 2-digit numbers. Be sure to start with one which is not divisible by 7.

Brain-stretcher! Why will the 6-digit number always be divisible by 7 even though the original number is not?

10.   More on Divisibility by 9   SUGGESTED GRADE SPAN—6, 7

You may want to review #2 in this chapter.

	Directions	*Example*
1.	Write any number which is *not* divisible by 9.	42168
2.	Find its digit sum.	21
3.	Find the number which, if added to the digit sum, gives a number which *is* divisible by 9.	$+\ 6$ / 27
4.	Form a 6-digit number by inserting this digit in front of your original.	642168
5.	Divide to see if that is divisible by 9.	71352
6.	Form a 6-digit number by inserting the digit at the end of your original.	421686
7.	Divide to see if that is divisible by 9.	46854

Will the result be divisible by 9 no matter where you insert the new digit you get in step 3?

Try this with several different original numbers with different numbers of digits.

11. Division Without Dividing

SUGGESTED GRADE
SPAN—6, 7

Suppose the division key on your calculator isn't working. Below is an example of how you can still divide with your calculator if you are careful.

Problem: 93,457 ÷ 386

Step 1:   93,457
         − 38,600 (100 × 386)
         ─────────
            54,857   ⎫
Step 2: − 38,600 (100 × 386) ⎬ 200
         ─────────   ⎭
            16,257
Step 3: −   3,860 (10 × 386)
         ─────────
            12,397
Step 4: −   3,860 (10 × 386) ⎫
         ─────────   ⎪
             8,537   ⎪
Step 5: −   3,860 (10 × 386) ⎬ 40
         ─────────   ⎪
             4,677   ⎪
Step 6: −   3,860 (10 × 386) ⎭
         ─────────
               817
Step 7: −   386 (1 × 386)   ⎫
         ─────────   ⎬ 2
               431   ⎭
Step 8: −   386 (1 × 386)
         ─────────
             ⑤⑤

The quotient will be $242^{R\ 45}$.

A quick way to do this without having to do any major writing is to keep a tally of your subtractions by place value, as shown in the example below:

H	T	O
//	////	//

Practice this division by subtraction with several examples. Stay with problems not greater than quotients in the hundreds until you can do them quickly. Then try some with greater quotients.

12. Tricky Three   SUGGESTED GRADE SPAN—6, 7

Directions	*Example*
1. Select any 2-digit number which is *not* divisible by 3.	47
2. Enter the 6-digit numeral formed by repeating these digits 3 times.	474747
3. Now divide to see if that number is divisible by 3.	158158

Try this for several different original 2-digit numbers. Be sure to use numbers not divisible by 3.

Brain-stretcher! Why will the 6-digit number be divisible by 3 even though the original number is not?

13. Divisibility by 6   SUGGESTED GRADE SPAN—7, 8

Do the problems on the chart below. One example is done for you.

Number	Divisible by 6?	Divisible by 2?	Divisible by 3?
624	Yes	Yes	Yes
429			
798			
5432			
3456			

Based on the results of the chart, what seems to be the rule for divisibility by 6? Check your theory by first predicting whether the numbers below are divisible by 6, then checking with your calculator.

a) 7,824   b) 67,816   c) 765,432

Brain-stretcher! Applying part of the concept above, predict the rule for divisibility by 12. Be careful to pick the most *efficient* way of testing.

14. Unique Problems   SUGGESTED GRADE SPAN—7, 8

Find the quotient in the problem below.

$$\frac{57,429}{6,381}$$

Look carefully at the digits of the problem. What do you observe?

Brain-stretcher! Can you find another division problem which is the same type of situation as this one?

15. More on Divisibility by 7   SUGGESTED GRADE SPAN—7, 8

We've seen in some earlier parts of this chapter (#7 and #8) certain ways of forming special numbers which will be divisible by 7. There are some other ways to do this, also.

a) Select any 1-digit number (8). Double it (16). Form the numeral you get by placing the second number in front of the first (168). Try this with several (all) 1-digit numbers to see if the result is always divisible by 7.

b) Select any 2-digit number (73). Triple it (219). Again, form a new numeral by placing the second in front of the first (21,973). Try this with several 2-digit numbers to see if the result is always divisible by 7.

c) According to the pattern above, we would expect to be able to get a number divisible by 7 by selecting any 3-digit number and multiplying it by 4. Try this to see if it works.

Brain-stretcher! Although we got an unexpected result in c above, apply the same pattern to a 4-digit number. (In some cases, you will not be able to do this on your calculator if you have only an 8-digit display). If you think it works, try a 5-digit number.

16. Divisibility by 11   SUGGESTED GRADE SPAN—8, 9

Look carefully at the examples below. Each number is divisible by 11.

a) 4 0 0 4

$4 + 0 = 4$
$0 + 4 = 4$

b) 2 7 1 4 8

$2 + 1 + 8 = 11$
$7 + 4 = 11$

c) 4 1 3 5 0 1

$4 + 3 + 0 = 7$
$1 + 5 + 1 = 7$

Can you describe a rule for checking divisibility by 11, based on what is shown in these examples? Test your theory by predicting whether the following are divisible by 11, then checking.

a) 5456   b) 89,871   c) 46,343   d) 135,795

17. Special Brain-Stretcher   SUGGESTED GRADE
                                         SPAN—9 AND UP

Explain why the rule for divisibility by 4 works. Try
to use an algebraic proof, if possible.

18. Special Brain-Stretcher B   SUGGESTED GRADE
                                           SPAN—9 AND UP

Prove the divisibility rule for 9.

SELECTED ANSWERS

1. A number is divisible by 3 if the sum of its digits is
   divisible by 3.

2. A number is divisible by 9 if the sum of its digits is
   divisible by 9. Every number that is divisible by 9 is
   also divisible by 3 because 9 is divisible by 3. However, not every number that is divisible by 3 is also
   divisible by 9 (e.g., 246).

3. Yes, it will always be divisible by 99. The only
   possible differences you can get when you subtract a
   3-digit number from its reverse (if not all digits are
   the same) are 99, 198, 297, 396, 495, 594, 693, 792
   and 891. These are 99×1, 99×2, etc.

4. $7 \times 11 \times 13 = 1001$. Any 3-digit number multiplied
   by 1001 is its tautonym. The 1000 in 1001 gives a
   product which shifts the digits 3 places to the left;
   the 1, of course, is the original. Therefore, any 6-digit

tautonym is divisible by 1001 and, therefore, by dividing by 7, 11, and 13 in any order, you get the original number.

5. A number is divisible by 4 if the numeral of its last 2 digits is a number divisible by 4. This is similar to the rule for 2, except in that rule we check only to see if the last digit is divisible by 2.

6. A number is divisible by 8 only if the numeral formed by its last 3 digits represents a number divisible by 8.

7. If you reread the solution for #4 above, you'll see that every 6-digit tautonym is divisible by 7.

8. a) BIG SHOE
    b) BEE GLEE
    c) OBOE HOBO
    d) O SOLO LEO

9. If you take any 6-digit numeral in this form (ababab) and divide it by the simple unrepeated value (ab), the result is always 10101. And 10101 is divisible by 7.

12. This is similar to #8. Again ababab divided by ab = 10101, and 10101 is divisible by 3.

Notice that the solution to this, as well as to 4, 7 and 8 above, is related to the multiplication tricks explained in #11 in Chapter 3!

13. A number is divisible by 6 *only if* it is divisible by both 2 and 3. The most efficient way to check is to see first if it is even (divisible by 2); only if it is, you then find the digit sum to see if it is divisible by 3, also. If both, then it is divisible by 6.

A similar rule applies to 12. Check first for divisibility by 4, using the rule in #5; then check for divisibility by 3. If both, then it is divisible by 12.

14. Each of the digits 1–9 is used exactly once in the problem, and the division works exactly. This will happen only for rare combinations of the digits. This may have taken many trials and errors! One possible solution is:

$$\frac{58{,}239}{6{,}471}$$

15. The pattern breaks down if you start with a 3-digit number. (Remember that a 3-digit number can be changed to a 6-digit number divisible by 7 by forming its tautonym.)

The pattern for an original 4-digit number would be to multiply it by 5, insert the result in front, then check for divisibility by 7.

$$\begin{array}{r} 3628 \\ \times\ 5 \\ \hline 18140 \end{array} \qquad \frac{181403628}{7} = 25914804$$

16. A number will be divisible by 11 if the sum of the digits in all of the odd-numbered positions (first + third + fifth, etc.) equals the sum of the digits in all of the even-numbered positions (second + fourth + sixth, etc.).

17. In any number the value of all of the digits to the left of the tens' place is divisible by 4. This is because their place values (100; 1,000; 10,000; etc.) are all divisible by 4. Therefore, the whole number will be divisible by 4 if the value of the last 2 places is. This can be put into the form of an algebraic proof rather easily. Try it.

18. For simplicity, the proof below will use a 4-digit numeral, with a–d representing the respective digits. Then the number is:

$$1000a + 100b + 10c + d$$
$$= (999 + 1)a + (99 + 1)b + (9 + 1)c + d$$
$$= 999a + 99b + 9c + (a + b + c + d)$$
$$= 9(111a + 11b + c) + (a + b + c + d)$$

Since the first expression will be divisible by 9 regardless of the values of a, b and c (because it has the factor 9), the whole number will be divisible by 9 *if and only if* the second term—a + b + c + d (the digit sum)—is also divisible by 9.

Chapter 6

Get the Point?

1. Decimal Palindromes

SUGGESTED GRADE
SPAN—5–7

In Chapter 2 (#3) you learned about palindromes—
numbers that read the same forward and backward.
You also discovered that there was a repeating addition process which, for most numbers, eventually
gave a palindrome. This is a similar activity.

There is one additional caution with decimal palindromes. You must also place the decimal point in the
correct position to make the trick work. Two examples are shown below:

a)
```
      9.31
   + 13.9
   ───────
     24.21
   + 12.42
   ───────
     36.63  (Palindrome)
```

b)
```
      897.3
   +     3.798
   ────────────
      901.098
   +  890.109
   ────────────
     1791.207
   +  702.1971
   ────────────
     2493.4041
   + 1404.3942
   ────────────
     3897.7983  (Palindrome)
```

79

Note that in decimal palindromes the decimal point must always be at the point where the "reversal" begins in the pattern.

Follow the process for the numbers below:

a) 7.9   (number of steps?
             decimal palindrome sum?)
b) 6.23   (number of steps?
             decimal palindrome sum?)
c) 57.81   (number of steps?
             decimal palindrome sum?)

Can you find another original decimal which requires at least four steps?

2. Decimal Magic Squares

SUGGESTED GRADE
SPAN—5–7

In Chapter 3 (#2) you learned about Magic Squares. You should reread the definition and look at the example. Decimal Magic Squares follow the same rules.

Find the missing numbers in the decimal magic squares below. The magic sum is given.

7.44		
		6.62
	8.26	

Magic Sum: 14.94

	4.71	3.02	
6.2			11.27
6.13		9.58	
		12.69	1.33

Magic Sum: 34.8

3. Upsy Daisy   SUGGESTED GRADE SPAN—5–7

In Chapter 1 (#15) you did some problems where the digits in the answer, read upside-down, spelled a message. Follow the same procedure in the problems below. (The decimal point separates words.)

a) What did the homeowner say to the panhandler who came to the door for a free meal? To answer, do: $625.9 + 178.16$. (You'll need to imagine a 0 at the beginning of the whole number part of the answer to get this one.)

b) What did the bashful teenage boy say when the young girl asked him for a date? To answer, do: $5928.30 - 1421.90$. (Do not omit the zeroes, or your message will be incomplete, but also move your decimal point to fixed 2 instead of floating!)

Remember to move your decimal point back to floating before proceeding.

Brain-stretcher! Try to make some similar word puzzles which have two-word answers with the decimal point separating the words.

4. The Magic of 1.1   SUGGESTED GRADE SPAN—6, 7

Use your calculator to complete the table below. One example is done.

$6.9 + 9.6 = 16.5$ $1.1 \times (6 + 9) = 16.5$		$8.2 + 2.8 =$ $1.1 \times (8 + 2) =$
$7.4 + 4.7 =$ $1.1 \times (7 + 4) =$		$3.5 + 5.3 =$ $1.1 \times (3 + 5) =$
$1.8 + 8.1 =$ $1.1 \times (1 + 8) =$		$2.3 + 3.2 =$ $1.1 \times (2 + 3) =$

What did you observe? Do you think this happens
in all cases, or are these special? Try the pattern with
23.4 + 4.32 and 1.1 × (23 + 4). Does the pattern
still hold?

Brain-stretcher! Can you show why the pattern works
for those numbers?

5. **The Magic of .9**   SUGGESTED GRADE SPAN—6, 7

Complete the table below in a similar way as you did
#4. Again, one example is done for you.

8.3 − 3.8 = 4.5 .9 × (8 − 3) = 4.5	7.6 − 6.7 = .9 × (7 − 6) =
9.4 − 4.9 = .9 × (9 − 4) =	3.1 − 1.3 = .9 × (3 − 1) =
8.2 − 2.8 = .9 × (8 − 2) =	9.6 − 6.9 = .9 × (9 − 6) =

What did you observe? Do you think it happens in
all cases, or are these special? Try the pattern with
23.4 − 4.32 and .9 × (23 − 4). Does the pattern
still hold?

Brain-stretcher! Can you show why the pattern works
for those numbers?

6. **Come Again?**   SUGGESTED GRADE SPAN—6–8

Use your calculator to do the first three conversions
below (change the fractions to decimals to 7 places).
Try to predict the rest of the answers before computing them; then check.

1/9 =
2/9 =
3/9 =
4/9 =
5/9 =
6/9 =
7/9 =
8/9 =

Based on the pattern you observed, what should be the decimal value *to* 7 *places* for 9/9? But what happens if you do 9/9 on your calculator? How do you account for this difference?

The type of decimal you get for these fractions is called a *repeating* decimal. There is a mathematical symbol—called the vinculum—used to express them. For example, .1111 . . . is written as .$\bar{1}$; the bar (vinculum) above the one means that the one repeats infinitely. This may help explain the problem with 9/9.

7. **99 Revisited B**   SUGGESTED GRADE SPAN—6–8

We've seen in several earlier chapters that 99 is a special number. Do the same thing with the list below that you did in #6.

1/99 =
2/99 =
3/99 =
4/99 =
5/99 =
6/99 =
7/99 =
8/99 =
9/99 =

Brain-stretcher! Can you write these answers the short way, using the vinculum? (Reread #6 if it helps you.)

8. 101 Revisited   SUGGESTED GRADE SPAN—6–8

We also learned some special things about 101 in earlier chapters. Do the same thing as before with these; remember to try to predict the last six on the list before using your calculator to check your predictions.

$1/101 =$
$2/101 =$
$3/101 =$
$4/101 =$
$5/101 =$
$6/101 =$
$7/101 =$
$8/101 =$
$9/101 =$

It may be a little more difficult to see the repeating pattern in these because the calculator "runs out of room." However, you can probably figure out what it will be. If so, try the:

Brain-stretcher! Can you write the answers for these with a vinculum?

9. Is It 11 or 9?   SUGGESTED GRADE SPAN—6–8

Notice how the numbers around 10, 100, etc. are special? We've had 9, 99, 101, and several others in different chapters. We also had .9 and 1.1 earlier in this chapter. See what happens with 11 as a denominator.

$1/11 =$
$2/11 =$
$3/11 =$
$4/11 =$
$5/11 =$
$6/11 =$
$7/11 =$
$8/11 =$
$9/11 =$

Why do you suppose this trick has the title it does?

Brain-stretcher! Can you write these answers with a vinculum?

10. Strange Seven   SUGGESTED GRADE SPAN—6–8

Do the same thing as with the other fraction lists.

$1/7 =$
$2/7 =$
$3/7 =$
$4/7 =$
$5/7 =$
$6/7 =$

It is much harder with this list than with any of the earlier ones to see the repeating pattern. If you did them correctly, the last digit on your display is the same as the tenths digit. If you could extend the division further, you'd find the others repeating in the same order.

Brain-stretcher! Try to write these answers with the vinculum.

We could continue with this type of list and get many more patterns. However, it may be more fun for you

to try to make up your own problems to see which
fractions give repeating decimals, and to see any
other patterns which may arise. Certainly some
denominators you may want to try include 13, 37,
999. We've seen in earlier chapters that these behave
in special ways.

11. Special Sums   SUGGESTED GRADE SPAN—6–8

For each pair of fraction sums below, find the decimal
equivalent for each fraction, then find the decimal
sum (to as many places as your display).

a) 1/21 + 1/42
b) 1/18 + 1/63
c) 1/15 + 1/210

What do you observe about the sum of each?

Now find the decimal value for 1/14. What do you
observe? What can you say about the fraction form
of the sums above?

Brain-stretcher! There is another pair of unit fractions
(fractions with 1 in the numerator) whose sum is
1/14 (or .0714285 on your display). Can you find
them? Hint: One is between 10 and 20; the other,
between 110 and 125.

12. Beyond Your Display   SUGGESTED GRADE
                                       SPAN—7–9

Some repeating decimals are difficult to discover with
a calculator because the digits don't start repeating
until after the seventh position. Since the calculator
doesn't extend any further, you can't see the pattern
easily.

The number of digits in the decimal of a repeating decimal determines its *period*. For example, the decimal equivalent of 1/37 is .027027027 . . . , or .$\overline{027}$. Because there are 3 digits which repeat (0, 2, and 7), the period is 3.

We will use the idea of period to find the decimal equivalents of some fractions which don't repeat until after the seventh place (or at it).

Find the decimal equivalents, to seven places, for the following fractions:

1/13 =	2/13 =
3/13 =	5/13 =
4/13 =	6/13 =
9/13 =	7/13 =
10/13 =	8/13 =
12/13 =	11/13 =

Look carefully at the first column. What do you observe about the digits of each answer? (You should see the same set of 6 digits in each and in a similar order, although each begins with a different one of the 6. Also, the 7th digit is the same as the first.)

Based on your observation, write the decimal equivalent for each as a repeating decimal, using the vinculum. Do the same for the fractions in the second column.

What is the period of each of these decimals?

(Actually, since these showed a beginning of a repeated pattern *in* the seventh position, rather than after, this is one of the easier to determine.)

13. Strange Sums   SUGGESTED GRADE SPAN—7–9

Because the repeating digits play tricks on us with the limited display of a calculator, it can be difficult to find the exact sum of two repeating decimals. Here, we can sometimes use our knowledge of fractions to help. Look at the examples below.

$$\begin{array}{r} 1/3 = .3333333\ldots \\ +\ 1/6 = .1666666\ldots \\ \hline = .4999999\ldots \end{array}$$

But we know that $1/3 + 1/6 = 1/2$.

What can we conclude about the fraction equivalent of $.4\overline{9}$, or $.4999999\ldots$?

Then what is the decimal sum of $.\overline{3} + .1\overline{6}$?

$$\begin{array}{r} 5/12 = .4166666\ldots \\ +\ 7/12 = .5833333\ldots \\ \hline .9999999\ldots \end{array}$$

But we know that $5/12 + 7/12 = 1$.

What can we then conclude about the fraction equivalent of $.\overline{9}$, or $.9999999\ldots$?

Use this idea to find the *exact decimal* sum of $1/15 + 2/15$.

14. Half a Loaf   SUGGESTED GRADE SPAN—7 AND UP

This puzzler should not be attempted unless you have lots of time and patience. We saw in Chapter 5 (#13) a special quotient which used each of the digits 1–9, the answer for which was 9. Therefore, the unit fraction 1/9 can be found by 6381/57429. Check to see if their decimal equivalents are the same.

There is also a fraction which uses each of the digits 1–9 exactly once which equals 1/2. Can you find it? (A hint to save some time—the numerator begins with 6; the denominator, with 1.)

15. More on Unit Fractions

SUGGESTED GRADE SPAN—7 AND UP

As mentioned earlier, unit fractions are fractions whose numerator is 1.

Some early civilizations never used anything but unit fractions. All other fractions were expressed as the sum of unit fractions. For example,

7/8 would be written as 1/2 + 1/4 + 1/8
2/7 would be written as 1/4 + 1/28

Find the unit fractions whose sum is the given fraction for each problem below, using decimal equivalents and your calculator, if necessary:

a) 2/11   (one 1-digit and one 2-digit denominator)
b) 2/99   (one 2-digit and one 3-digit denominator)
c) 4/7   (one 1-digit and one 2-digit denominator)
d) 5/18   (two 1-digit denominators)

16. Adding Repeating Decimals

SUGGESTED GRADE SPAN—7 AND UP

You saw some special sums of repeating decimals in #13. Many repeating decimals can be added if you know how to line them up. Look at the examples below, which list them to seven places and show the use of the vinculum:

a) $.6843434\ldots = .68\overline{43}$
     $+\,.2516161\ldots = +\,.25\overline{16}$
      $.9359595\ldots = .93\overline{59}$

These have the same period and begin repeating in the same place.

b) $.6842323\ldots = .684\overline{23} =$
     $+\,.9359595\ldots = +\,.93\overline{59}$
      1.5191919

$.684\overline{23}$
$+\,.935\overline{95}$
$1.519\overline{19}$ or $1.5\overline{19}$

Note that in this example we have to "slide" the vinculum to begin one place later in the second number to line up repeating digits. It does not change the decimal value. These have the same period (2), but do not repeat in the same initial place. Also note that the final 9 in the first part of the example represents what the value would be from adding $2 + 9$ in the next (missing) eighth place.

c) $.6666666\ldots = .\overline{666}$
     $+\,.4184184\ldots \quad +\,.\overline{418}$
      $1.0850850 \quad\quad 1.\overline{085}$

These have a different period. Just extend the repeat of the first to comply.

Now find the sums of the repeating decimals below:

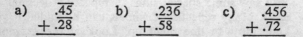

a) $.\overline{45}$ b) $.2\overline{36}$ c) $.\overline{456}$
   $+\,.\overline{28}$ $+\,.5\overline{8}$ $+\,.\overline{72}$

17. **Subtracting Repeating Decimals** SUGGESTED GRADE

SPAN—7 AND UP

The same general techniques used in adding repeating decimals can also be applied to subtraction. See if you can incorporate them to do the problems below.

a) $\overline{.45}$ b) $.5\overline{36}$ c) $\overline{.72}$
   $-.28$ $-.28$ $-.2\overline{34}$

Brain-stretcher! Can you devise a way to multiply repeating decimals? If so, try one which you can check by equivalent fractions, such as $.\overline{3} \times .1\overline{6}$ (1/3 × 1/6).

18. **More about Fibonacci** SUGGESTED GRADE

SPAN—9 AND UP

In Chapter 2 (#14) the pattern of a general Fibonacci-type series or sequence was described. The basic sequence of Fibonacci numbers is:

1, 1, 2, 3, 5, 8, 13, 21, 34, 55, 89, 144, 233, . . .

By finding decimal equivalents of the fractions formed by adjacent numbers in the sequence, we can observe a pattern. The first few are done for you. Do the rest.

1/1	=	1.
2/1	=	2.
3/2	=	1.5
5/3	=	
8/5	=	
13/8	=	
21/13	=	
34/21	=	
55/34	=	
89/55	=	
144/89	=	
233/144	=	

You should notice something beginning to happen. You can see that the quotients beyond this point will almost certainly begin with 1.61. Use the procedure for extending the sequence about ten more places. Then find the quotient of the last number divided by the preceding one for each additional pair you've formed.

What value now begins to appear for each fraction? We describe such a situation by saying that this process is converging on that value.

SELECTED ANSWERS

1. a) 37.73 (three steps)
   b) 38.83 (one step)
   c) 174.471 (three steps)

The brain-stretcher, of course, has many possible solutions. The value 28.71 takes 6 steps to get 615.516.

2. a)

7.44	1.7	5.8
3.34	4.98	6.62
4.16	8.26	2.52

b)

16.07	4.71	3.02	11
6.2	7.82	9.51	11.27
6.13	7.89	9.58	11.2
6.4	14.38	12.69	1.33

3. a) GO HOBO
   b) OH GOSH

4. It works for all problems in the form $a.b + b.a$ (= $1.1 \times (a + b)$).

Proof: $(a + .1b) + (b + .1a)$
$= 1.1a + 1.1b$
$= 1.1(a + b)$

It does not work for examples not in this pattern.

5. It works for all problems in the form a.b — b.a $(= .9 \times (a - b))$.

Proof: $(a + .1b) - (b + .1a)$
$= .9a - .9b$
$= .9(a - b)$

It does not work for examples not in this pattern.

6. By pattern, the decimal value of 9/9, to seven places, is .9999999. However, 9/9 also equals 1. This is because the 9's repeat infinitely, which (if we could actually reach it) would become 1.

7. $1/99 = .\overline{01}$ $2/99 = .\overline{02}$ $3/99 = .\overline{03}$ etc.

8. $1/101 = .\overline{0099}$ $2/101 = .\overline{0198}$ $3/101 = .\overline{0297}$ etc.

9. As with 101, where we get multiples of 99 in a pattern, division by 11 gives multiples of 9 in a pattern. (Notice that division by 9 gives a form of multiples of 11; division by 99 gives a form of multiples of 101. These numbers which are either 1 greater or 1 less than the powers of 10 are truly special and interrelated!)

10. $1/7 = .\overline{142857}$ $3/7 = .\overline{428571}$ $5/7 = .\overline{714285}$
    $2/7 = .\overline{285714}$ $4/7 = .\overline{571428}$ $6/7 = .\overline{857142}$

Notice that once you are aware that the same 6 digits repeat in order, but with a different initial digit each time, you can find all the remaining values but just starting with the next larger digit in the set. That is, since 1/7 began with 1 and 2/7 with 2, the 3/7 must begin with the 4, etc.

11. The decimal sum for each set, to the seven places on your display, will be .0714285. This is the same value you get for 1/14 on your display. Thus, the fraction sum of each set is 1/14.

Note: The actual value of 1/14 is $.0\overline{714285}$. You would know it had to be a repeating decimal because the 1/18 in problem b has a repeating 5.

Brain-stretcher: $1/16 + 1/112$

12. $1/13 = .\overline{076932}$ $2/13 = .\overline{153846}$
    $3/13 = .\overline{230769}$ $5/13 = .\overline{384615}$
    $4/13 = .\overline{307692}$ $6/13 = .\overline{461538}$
    $9/13 = .\overline{692307}$ $7/13 = .\overline{538461}$
    $10/13 = .\overline{769230}$ $8/13 = .\overline{615384}$
    $12/13 = .\overline{923076}$ $11/13 = .\overline{846153}$

Note that as in number 10, once you know the 6 repeating digits for each of the two sets, you can find remaining values in the set by choosing the next larger digit of the set of 6 for each successive fraction. So in the Column A set, where the digit values are 0, 2, 3, 6, 7 and 9, those are the respective first digits of the decimals in the set.

The period is 6.

13. $.4\overline{9} = .5$ $\overline{.9} = 1$

$$1/15 = .0666666\ldots$$
$$+\ 2/15 = .1333333\ldots$$
$$.1999999\ldots = .2$$

(Note that $1/15 + 2/15 = 3/15$, or $1/5$, which is .2.)

14. 6729/13458

15. a) $1/6 + 1/66$
b) $1/90 + 1/110$
c) $1/2 + 1/14$
d) $1/6 + 1/9$

16. a) $.\overline{73}$ b) $.8\overline{2}$ c) $1.\overline{183729}$
(You may have $1.\overline{183}$.)

17. a) $.\overline{17}$ b) $.2\overline{53}$ c) $.\overline{493038}$
(You may have $.\overline{493}$.)

18. The values seem to be converging on 1.6180339.

Chapter 7

X-Tensions

1. A Squaring Trick   SUGGESTED GRADE SPAN—6, 7

Note: For all activities in this chapter which involve squaring you will want to know the quickest way on your calculator. Of course, you could do the square of 8 by pressing, in turn, 8; ×; 8; =. However, on many calculators you can get the answer by pressing 8; ×; =. Try yours to see which way to do it.

Directions	*Example*
1. Select any number.	37
2. Square it.	1369
3. Square the next greater number (38^2).	1444
4. Find the positive difference.	75
5. Subtract 1.	74
6. Multiply by 1/2.	37

Try this for several different original numbers. What always happens?

Brain-stretcher! Can you prove algebraically why this always happens? (It requires the ability to square a binomial, so you need algebra.)

2. A Fraction Squaring Trick   SUGGESTED GRADE SPAN—6, 7

Find the squares of each fraction shown below. You can work with decimals on your calculator, then convert the final answer back to fraction form.

a) 6 1/2   b) 9 1/2   c) 15 1/2   d) 99 1/2

Now do:
a) 6 × 7   b) 9 × 10
c) 15 × 16   d) 99 × 100

Brain-stretcher! Can you describe a quick way to square a mixed numeral whose fraction is 1/2 without long work?

3. Some Special Squares
SUGGESTED GRADE
SPAN—6, 7

Find the four values in each column below.

$3^2 =$ $9^2 =$
$33^2 =$ $99^2 =$
$333^2 =$ $999^2 =$
$3333^2 =$ $9999^2 =$

What do you notice when you compare results in the two columns?

Brain-stretcher! Predict the values of $333,333^2$ and $999,999^2$.

4. Another Squaring Trick
SUGGESTED GRADE
SPAN—6, 7

Example

1. Select any number ending in 5.   125
2. Take the number formed by the
   other digits without the 5.   12
3. Multiply it by the next greater (13).   156
4. Affix 25 to the end of this.   15625

That number is the square of the original. Try it with several numbers.

5. Patterns of Powers   SUGGESTED GRADE SPAN—6, 7

Complete each of the columns below.

a) $1^2 - 0^2 =$ b) $2^2 - 0^2 =$ c) $3^2 - 0^2 =$
$2^2 - 1^2 =$ $3^2 - 1^2 =$ $4^2 - 1^2 =$
$3^2 - 2^2 =$ $4^2 - 2^2 =$ $5^2 - 2^2 =$

At this point you should be able to extend each column, knowing both what the problems should be and predicting the answers. Try to extend each three more positions. Describe the patterns in your own words.

Brain-stretcher! Do you know what the next column, if there were one, would be? Do the first three problems of such a column, then predict the fourth answer and check it.

Brain-stretcher! Can you show the pattern of the three columns above algebraically?

6. More Patterns with Powers   SUGGESTED GRADE SPAN—6, 7

Reminder: The cube of a number is found by using it as a factor three times. For example, $4^3 = 4 \times 4 \times 4 = 64$.

Every cube can be expressed as the difference of two squares. In fact, there is a pattern in the squares used to express consecutive cubes. Try to complete the table below, in each case using the difference of two squares. The first is done for you.

$1^3 = 1 - 0 = 1^2 - 0^2$
$2^3 =$
$3^3 =$
$4^3 =$
$5^3 =$
$6^3 =$
$7^3 =$
$8^3 =$
$9^3 =$

Brain-stretcher! The fourth powers of numbers can also be expressed as the difference of two squares. Can you find the values for 1^4 through 5^4, expressing each as the difference of two squares?

7. A Special Triangle   SUGGESTED GRADE SPAN—6, 7

Examine the triangle below.

$$
\begin{array}{c}
1 \\
3 \quad 5 \\
7 \quad 9 \quad 11 \\
13 \quad 15 \quad 17 \quad 19 \\
21 \quad 23 \quad 25 \quad 27 \quad 29
\end{array}
$$

Find the sum in each row. What pattern do you see?

Brain-stretcher! Assuming the pattern holds, what will be the sum in the tenth row? (If you have time, extend the triangle that far and check.)

8. A Special Triangle Extended   SUGGESTED GRADE SPAN—6, 7

Use the triangle from #7 for this activity, also. Complete the table; this time the third is done to be sure you see the pattern.

Rows Used	Sum
1	
1,2	
1,2,3	36
1,2,3,4	
1,2,3,4,5	

What pattern do you see in these sums?

Brain-stretcher! Assuming the pattern holds, what will be the sum if you add rows 1–10? (If you have time, extend the triangle that far and check.)

9. Squares with Squares   SUGGESTED GRADE SPAN—6, 7

First test the equation below to see if it is true.

$$3^2 + 6^2 + 7^2 = 2^2 + 3^2 + 9^2$$

Now check each problem below to see if it is also true.

a) $32^2 + 63^2 + 79^2 = 23^2 + 36^2 + 97^2$
b) $33^2 + 69^2 + 72^2 = 33^2 + 96^2 + 27^2$
c) $39^2 + 62^2 + 73^2 = 93^2 + 26^2 + 37^2$
d) $32^2 + 69^2 + 73^2 = 23^2 + 96^2 + 37^2$
e) $33^2 + 62^2 + 79^2 = 33^2 + 26^2 + 97^2$
f) $39^2 + 63^2 + 72^2 = 93^2 + 36^2 + 27^2$

What can you conclude from this?

Brain-stretcher! Can you find another set of six 1-digit squares that work like the original? If so, set up one set of 2-digit sums like those in the table to see if it also works.

10. The Magic of 153   SUGGESTED GRADE SPAN—6, 7

Directions	*Example*
1. Select any multiple of 3.	81
2. Cube each of its digits.	512; 1
3. Add the results.	513
4. Cube each of those digits.	125;1;27
5. Add the results.	153

This process always results, *eventually*, in 153. Be careful, though, because some numbers take many steps.

What happens when you use the process with 153 as the number?

11. Automorphs   SUGGESTED GRADE SPAN—6, 7

Find the value of each expression below:

$$5^2 =$$
$$6^2 =$$
$$25^2 =$$
$$76^2 =$$
$$376^2 =$$
$$625^2 =$$
$$9376^2 =$$

What is unusual about the results? These seven numbers are called automorphs because of their unusual squares.

12. Another Cube Caper   SUGGESTED GRADE SPAN—6, 7

Directions	*Example*
1. Select any number not divisible by 7.	142
2. Cube that number.	2,863,288
3. Add 1 to the result.	2,863,289
4. See if that is divisible by 7.	No
5. If not, subtract 1 from the result in step 2.	2,863,287
6. Divide by 7.	409,041

Try this with several original numbers. What do you observe?

13. Making a Million SUGGESTED GRADE SPAN—6, 7

There are many interesting problems you can do focusing on one million. A few are listed below. You may want to try some others which you make up yourself.

a) A million seconds is equal to how many days?
b) A million minutes is equal to how many years?
c) A million inches is equal to how many miles? (Notice how easy this kind of problem would be in the Metric System!)
d) If you are paid $100 a week for 50 weeks a year, how long will it take you to earn $1,000,000?

14. Family Tree SUGGESTED GRADE SPAN—7, 8

Count yourself as the latest generation in your family tree. You can be represented as 2^0, or 1 person. (Remember that any number raised to the 0 power, except 0, equals 1.) You, of course, have two immediate ancestors—your mother and father. That total represents 2^1. Since each of them had two parents (you had four grandparents), the total in that generation is 2^2. Continuing this idea, how many ancestors did you have in the tenth preceding generation?

Brain-stretcher! How many total ancestors did you have in all of the preceding generations through and including the tenth?

Brain-stretcher! Based on your answer to the previous question and assuming 25 years to a generation, how many generations must pass before you accumulate over 25,000 descendants? How many years?

15. Finding Square Roots

Here is a procedure you can use to find square roots
with your calculator, assuming you don't have a special calculator with a square-root key. The first
example with the directions is done for you.

Directions	*Example*
1. Enter the number whose square root you want to find.	3364
2. Make a guess as to its square root. (The more intelligent your guess, the fewer steps you will require.)	52
3. Divide the original by your guess.	64.7
4. Find the average of your guess and the quotient: $1/2(52 + 64.7)$	58.35
5. Divide the original by the result.	57.65
6. Average steps 4 and 5: $1/2(58.35 + 57.65)$.	58
7. Divide the original by the result.	58

The process would be continued until the result of
averaging is equal to the result of dividing to as many
places as you require your answer. In this example,
$\sqrt{3364} = 58$.

This was an example where the original number had
an exact square root. Most numbers do not. Usually,
you want the square root to two or three decimal
places for practical purposes.

Find the square roots below to at least two decimal
places:

a) $\sqrt{2209} =$ b) $\sqrt{1250} =$

c) $\sqrt{4000} =$ d) $\sqrt{3.24}$

Brain-stretcher! What did the bashful teenage boy say to the girl who asked him for a date? To find out, find the square root of 5,475,600 and hold your display to a mirror.

16. A Trick with Square Roots

SUGGESTED GRADE
SPAN—7, 8

Directions	*Example*
1. Select 2 numbers, p and q, so the q is 5 more than p.	8; 13
2. Square p.	64
3. Square q.	169
4. Add the two results.	233
5. Double the sum.	466
6. Subtract 25.	441
7. Find the square root (should be a whole number).	21
8. Subtract 5.	16
9. Take 1/2; that's p; + 5 gives q.	8; 13

Brain-stretcher! Can you show an algebraic proof for why this works?

17. Another Square Root Trick

SUGGESTED GRADE
SPAN—7, 8

Directions	*Example*
1. Select 2 numbers, p and q, so that q is 2 more than p.	9; 11
2. Multiply.	99
3. Add 1.	100
4. Find the square root (a whole number).	10
5. Subtract 1: this gives p; + 2 is q.	9; 11

Brain-stretcher! Can you show algebraically why this works? This proof is easier than the one for #16, so most algebra 1 students can probably do it.

18. A Square Root Pattern   SUGGESTED GRADE SPAN—7, 8

Complete the first three lines of the table below. Then predict what the remainder will be. Check your prediction.

$$1 + 2 + 1 = ?; \sqrt{?} = ??$$
$$1 + 2 + 3 + 2 + 1 = ?; \sqrt{?} = ??$$
$$1 + 2 + 3 + 4 + 3 + 2 + 1 = ?; \sqrt{?} = ??$$
$$1 + 2 + 3 + 4 + 5 + 4 + 3 + 2 + 1 = ?; \sqrt{?} = ??$$

Continue both the left and right sides.

19. Power of the Fifth   SUGGESTED GRADE SPAN—7, 8

Complete the table below:

$1^5 =$

$2^5 =$

$3^5 =$

$4^5 =$

$5^5 =$

$6^5 =$

$7^5 =$

$8^5 =$

$9^5 =$

What do you observe about the final digit of each fifth power? Can you predict anything about the fifth power of every number? Test your guess by finding the fifth powers of some 2-digit numbers.

Brain-stretcher! What is the greatest 2-digit number whose fifth power you can find on your display case (if it's 8 places)?

20. Factorial Fun SUGGESTED GRADE SPAN—7, 8

The exclamation point has a special meaning as a mathematics symbol. When the exclamation point appears after a number N, it means you multiply all the factors $N(N - 1)(N - 2) \ldots \times 1$. For example, the expression 4! (read "four factorial") means $4 \times 3 \times 2 \times 1 = 24$.

Find the values of 1! through 10! on your calculator. Try to find a shortcut to save time.

Brain-stretcher! Suppose you are making 5-digit license plates in which you can use any of the digits 0–9, but no digit may appear more than once. How many different license plates can you make?

21. Magic Squares Revisited SUGGESTED GRADE SPAN—8, 9

Below is a magic square which shows how you can construct any 4×4 magic square from any original numbers.

$x+y+z+w$	$x-y-z+w$	$x-y-z$	$x+y+z-2w$
$x-y+z-2w$	$x+y-z$	$x+y-z+w$	$x-y+z+w$
$x+y-z-w$	$x-y+z-w$	$x-y+z$	$x+y-z+2w$
$x-y-z+2w$	$x+y+z$	$x+y+z-w$	$x-y-z-w$

Select any four values you wish for x, y, z, and w. You can include negative numbers, decimals, etc. Compute the value of each cell, using the formulas. Then check your results to see if you do have a magic square. (If you don't, recheck your cell calculations.)

Brain-stretcher! What will the magic sum of this square always be?

22. An Integer Magic Square

SUGGESTED GRADE
SPAN—8, 9

Complete the magic square below. Make the magic sum — 26.

1			−11
−13	−4	−8	
	−5		0
		−3	−14

23. Another Square Root Method

SUGGESTED GRADE
SPAN—8, 9

There is another method for finding square roots *if* the original number is a whole number perfect square. Just subtract consecutive odd natural numbers (1, 3, 5, . . .) until you reach 0. The number of subtractions you do is the value of the square root.

The example is for $\sqrt{121}$:

```
    121
  −   1        1
    120
  −   3        2
    117
  −   5        3
    112
  −   7        4
    105
  −   9        5
     96
  −  11        6
     85
  −  13        7
     72
  −  15        8
     57
  −  17        9
     40
  −  19       10
     21
  −  21       11
```

So $\sqrt{121} = 11$.

Try this process with several perfect squares. You should not need to do any writing other than keeping a tally of the number of subtractions you make.

Brain-stretcher! Try to devise a continuing subtraction pattern that will give you the cube root of a perfect whole number cube. If you try a few different patterns with the first few (8, 27, and 64), you should be able to find it.

24. Generating Consecutive Integers SUGGESTED GRADE
SPAN—9 AND UP

The algebraic expression $23x + 28y$ can be used to
generate consecutive integers. Look at the first two
examples below:

a) If $23x + 28y = 1$, integer values which work are
$x = 11, y = -9$.

$(23 \times 11) + [(28 \times (-9)] = 1$

b) To generate 2, we simply insert 2 as an additional
factor:

$[23 \times (11 \times 2)] + [28 \times (-9 \times 2)] = 2.$

Show how 3 and 4 are generated. Test the results on
your calculator.

25. Happy Easter SUGGESTED GRADE SPAN—9 AND UP

There is a lengthy algebraic process which will enable
you to compute the date on which Easter will fall in
any year. The one thing you must do carefully is find
remainders, since the calculator does not give them
directly. You can either multiply the quotient whole
number by the divisor and subtract from the dividend,
or try to use the decimal part of the quotient.

The calculation below is for the year 1977.

Directions	Example
1. year/19 = R, remainder A	R = 104, A = 1
2. year/100 = B, remainder C	B = 19, C = 77
3. B/4 = D, remainder E	D = 4, E = 3
4. (B + 8)/25 = F (omit remainder)	F = 1

5. $(B + 1 - F)/3 = G$
   (omit remainder) $\qquad G = 6$
6. $(19A + B + 15 - D - G)30 = $ (omit),
   remainder H $\qquad H = 10$
7. $C/4 = J$, remainder K $\qquad J = 19, \quad K = 1$
8. $(2E + 2J + 32 - H - K)/7 = $ omit,
   remainder M $\qquad M = 2$
9. $(A + 11H + 22M)/451 = N$ (omit remainder) $\qquad N = 0$
10. $(H + M + 114 - 7N)/31 = P$, remainder Q $\qquad P = 4, \quad Q = 2$

Month $= P \qquad P = 4$; 4th month is April
Date $= Q \qquad Q = 2$

Therefore, in 1977 Easter will be April 2.

Brain-stretcher! Compute the date for Easter in 1978.
You can probably check your answer with a calendar.

26. **Pythagorean Playground** SUGGESTED GRADE
SPAN—10, 11

Complete the table below.

a	b	c	a^2	b^2	$a^2 + b^2$	c^2
3	4	5				
5	12	13				
7	24	25				
8	15	17				
9	40	41				

What do you observe about the values in the last two columns? You probably recognize this now as the Pythagorean Theorem. When the relationship holds, you know definitely that the triangle is a right triangle.

The integral values used in the table are rare examples. In most cases, if you choose a and b randomly, the value for c will be irrational: a nonending, nonrepeating decimal. Select a few values at random to test this.

There are other integral values which will work, however. They can be found by simply using multiples of the sets in the original table. For example, if 3—4—5 is a right triangle, so is 6—8—10; 9—12—15; etc. Try some multiples for some of the sets in the original table to test this statement.

27. This Is the Limit!   SUGGESTED GRADE SPAN—11, 12

Find the sums below:

$1/2 + 1/4 =$
$1/2 + 1/4 + 1/8 =$
$1/2 + 1/4 + 1/8 + 1/16 =$
$1/2 + 1/4 + 1/8 + 1/16 + 1/32 =$
$1/2 + 1/4 + 1/8 + 1/16 + 1/32 + 1/64 =$
$1/2 + 1/4 + 1/8 + 1/16 + 1/32 + 1/64 + 1/128 =$
$1/2 + 1/4 + 1/8 + 1/16 + 1/32 + 1/64 + 1/128 + 1/256 =$

What do you notice about the results? If it were possible to extend this infinitely many times, what would the sum be?

Brain-stretcher! Express this infinite geometric series as a function and find its sum.

28. More on Unit Fractions #2   SUGGESTED GRADE
                                          SPAN—11, 12

In Chapter 6 (#15) there was a challenge to express
certain given fractions as the sum of unit fractions.
There are certain shortcuts for doing this. One is the
half-next plan and can be used when the denominator
of the given fraction is odd and the numerator is 2.
For example:

Directions	Example
1. Select a fraction of this type.	2/7
2. Add 1 to the denominator.	8
3. Take 1/2; call that D.	4
4. One fraction will be 1/D.	1/4
5. The other will be 1/(D × original denominator).	1/28

First check to see that $1/4 + 1/28$ does equal 2/7.
Then find the unit fractions which work to equal
2/19.

Brain-stretcher! Can you show algebraically why this
works?

29. The Golden Ratio   SUGGESTED GRADE SPAN—11, 12

The ancient geometers and architects had a ratio for
the length of a rectangle to its width for which the
most attractive dimensions of a building were used.
This value, called the Golden Ratio, is approximately
1.6180. (Where have you encountered that value
earlier in the book?)

If the length of a building were to be 247.2 meters,
what should its height (width of the "front" rectangle)
be to get maximum eye appeal?

You may want to do some additional reading on the Golden Ratio, including its many occurrences in nature. One example, the starfish, is shown below. Note the ratio 8/5 = 1.6, which is quite close.

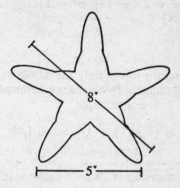

30. Lower Bounds   SUGGESTED GRADE SPAN—11, 12

In #27 we saw an example of an upper bound of a series. In that case, the upper bound was actually the sum of the series. The illustration below will be of a lower bound. Do the first three problems of the set:

$2/3 + 3/2 =$
$3/4 + 4/3 =$
$4/5 + 5/4 =$

Based on this limited number of cases, what appears to be the lower bound? Try a few more steps to be sure.

Brain-stretcher! Can you prove algebraically that that value is, in fact, the lower bound?

SELECTED ANSWERS

1. Let N be the first number. Then $N + 1$ is the next.

$$1/2 (N + 1)^2 - N^2 - 1$$
$$= 1/2(N^2 + 2N + 1 - N^2 - 1)$$
$$= 1/2(2N)$$
$$= N$$

2. The shortcut is to multiply the whole number part of the mixed numeral by the next greater whole number; then affix 1/4. For example,

$$(6 \ 1/2)^2 = (6 \times 7) + 1/4 = 42 \ 1/4$$

3. Each, of course, has its own pattern. It is interesting to note, however, that the pattern of both contains only the digits 0, 1, 8 and 9.

$$333,333^2 = 11,111,088,889$$
$$999,999^2 = 99,999,800,001$$

5.

$4^2 - 3^2 = 7$	$5^2 - 3^2 = 16$	$6^2 - 3^2 = 27$
$5^2 - 4^2 = 9$	$6^2 - 4^2 = 20$	$7^2 - 4^2 = 33$
$6^2 - 5^2 = 11$	$7^2 - 5^2 = 24$	$8^2 - 5^2 = 39$

The next column would be:
$$4^2 - 0^2 = 16$$
$$5^2 - 1^2 = 24$$
$$6^2 - 2^2 = 32 \quad \text{etc.}$$

Proof for column a:
$$N^2 - (N-1)^2 = N^2 - (N^2 - 2N + 1) = 2N - 1$$
Proof for column b:
$$N^2 - (N-2)^2 = N^2 - (N^2 - 4N + 4) = 4N - 4$$
Proof for column c:
$$N^2 - (N-3)^2 = N^2 - (N^2 - 6N + 9) = 6N - 9$$

6. $2^3 = 3^2 - 1^2$ $5^3 = 15^2 - 10^2$ $8^3 = 36^2 - 28^2$
$3^3 = 6^2 - 3^2$ $6^3 = 21^2 - 15^2$ $9^3 = 45^2 - 36^2$
$4^3 = 10^2 - 6^2$ $7^3 = 28^2 - 21^2$

Those who are familiar with triangular numbers will recognize the pattern. The triangular numbers are 1, 3, 6, 10, 15, ... This is determined by counting the total number of dots in a triangle formed by adding additional dots in each row. A diagram is shown below.

etc.

$1^4 = 1^2 - 0^2$
$2^4 = 5^2 - 3^2$
$3^4 = 15^2 - 12^2$
$4^4 = 20^2 - 12^2$
$5^4 = 65^2 - 60^2$

7.

Row	Sum	Pattern
1	1	1^3
2	8	2^3
3	27	3^3
4	64	4^3
5	125	5^3

The sum in the tenth row will be 10^3, or 1,000.

8.

Rows Used	Sum
1	1
1,2	9
1,2,3	36
1,2,3,4	100
1,2,3,4,5	225

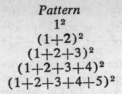

Pattern

$$1^2$$
$$(1+2)^2$$
$$(1+2+3)^2$$
$$(1+2+3+4)^2$$
$$(1+2+3+4+5)^2$$

The sum for rows 1–10 will be $(1 + 2 + 3 + \dots + 10)^2 = 55^2$
$$= 3025.$$

9. a) Both sides equal 11,234.
   b) Both sides equal 11,034.
   c) Both sides equal 10,694.
   d) Both sides equal 11,114.
   e) Both sides equal 11,174.
   f) Both sides equal 10,674.

If the sums of the squares of the three 1-digit numbers on each side of the original are equal, the sums of the squares of the three 2-digit numbers on each side formed by using all combinations of the original left and right, then reversing, will also be equal.

One other set which works is $4^2 + 5^2 + 6^2 = 2^2 + 3^2 + 8^2$. There is at least one other.

10. $1^3 + 5^3 + 3^3 = 1 + 125 + 27 = 153$; the cycle will keep generating 153.

11. Each original number being squared occurs as the final digit(s) of its actual square. For example, $9376^2 = 87,909,376$.

12. If any number not divisible by 7 is cubed, the value which is either 1 greater *or* 1 less than that cube will be divisible by 7.

13. a) 11.6   b) 1.9   c) 15.7   d) 200 years

14. In the tenth preceding generation you had 1,024 ancestors. In all of the generations through and including the tenth preceding you had 2,046 ancestors. You have to go to the 14th generation, or 350 years.

15. a) 47   b) 35.35   c) 63.25   d) 1.8

$\sqrt{5,475,600} = 2340$. If you hold this display to a mirror, the message will read, "O Yes."

16. The numbers will be presented by p and (p + 5) since q is 5 greater.

2. p^2
3. $q^2 = (p + 5)^2 = p^2 + 10p + 25$
4. $2p^2 + 10p + 25$
5. $4p^2 + 20p + 50$
6. $4p^2 + 20p + 25 = (2p + 5)^2$
7. $2p + 5$
8. $2p$
9. p

17. Let p represent the first number and p + 2 the second (q is 2 more):

2. $p(p + 2) = p^2 + 2p$
3. $p^2 + 2p + 1 = (p + 1)^2$
4. $p + 1$
5. p

18. The sums are 4, 9, 16, 25, 36, 49, 64, and 81. The respective square roots, of course, are 2, 3, 4, 5, 6, 7, 8 and 9—the middle numbers in the addition expressions.

19. The final digit of the fifth power of each single digit is the same as the digit itself. Therefore, the fifth power of any number will end in the same digit that ends the original number (e.g., the fifth power of 23 must end in 3). Note that $23^5 = 6,436,343$.

The greatest 2-digit number whose fifth power you can find on the calculator is 39; $39^5 = 90,224,199$.

20. The shortcut is quick. Once you've computed the value of 5! ($5 \times 4 \times 3 \times 2 \times 1$) to be 120, for instance, just multiply the 120 by 6 to get the value (720) of 6! ($6 \times 5 \times 4 \times 3 \times 2 \times 1$). To get 7!, multiply the 720 by 7; etc.

Brain-stretcher. You can make 30,240 license plates: $10 \times 9 \times 8 \times 7 \times 6$.

21. The magic sum will be 4x. An addition of any four related cells will show this:

$$\begin{aligned}
& x + y + z + w \\
+\ & x - y - z + w \\
+\ & x - y - z \\
+\ & x + y + z - 2w \\
\hline
& 4x
\end{aligned}$$

22.

1	−10	−6	−11
−13	−4	−8	−1
−12	−5	−9	0
−2	−7	−3	−14

23. The pattern is difficult to observe. If you tried it for 8, 27, and 64, you would note that you subtract 1,

7, 19, and 37. The formula for these is not easy to discover. It is $3n^2 - 3n + 1$ for $n = 1, 2, 3, \ldots$ to as many subtractions as necessary. It is, of course, a very inefficient method because you must first compute the numbers to be subtracted. However, if you don't have a cube-root table, it may help.

24. $23 \times (11 \times 3) + 28 \times (-9 \times 3) = 3$
$23 \times (11 \times 4) + 28 \times (-9 \times 4) = 4$

25. In 1978 Easter will fall on March 23.

27. The sum of the infinite series is 1. The series can be represented by:

$$\sum_{x=1,\infty} \frac{1}{2^x} = 1$$

28. $2/19 = 1/10 + 1/190$

The form of the original fraction for which the next-half process works is: $2/(2N - 1)$.

$$\frac{2}{2N - 1} = \frac{N}{N} = \frac{2N}{N(2N - 1)}$$

$$= \frac{2N - 1 + 1}{N(2N - 1)}$$

$$= \frac{2N - 1}{N(2N - 1)} + \frac{1}{N(2N - 1)}$$

$$= \frac{1}{N} + \frac{1}{N(2N - 1)}$$

29. 152.8 meters

30. They must all exceed 2 (the lower bound). The proof follows:

$$\frac{a}{a+1} + \frac{a+1}{a} = \frac{a}{a} \cdot \frac{a}{a+1} + \frac{a+1}{a} \cdot \frac{a+1}{a+1}$$

$$= \frac{2a^2 + 2a + 1}{a^2 + a}$$

$$= \frac{2(a^2 + a) + 1}{a^2 + a}$$

$$= 2 + \frac{1}{a^2 + a}$$

Since $a > 0$, $a^2 + a > 0$, and fraction > 0.

SECTION II

Games and Game-Puzzles

Chapter 8

Solitaires

All games and game-puzzles in this chapter are for one player and require only one calculator.

1. High Roller   SUGGESTED GRADE SPAN—4, 5

Additional materials needed: pair of dice; slips of bonus paper

Object: To cross out all the numbers 1–9 before making a throw which has no combination

Rules:
1. Write the numerals 1–9 on a sheet of paper.
2. Roll the dice. Find the total dots shown.
3. You may cross out that number or any combination of numbers which has that total. For example, suppose you roll a 9. You may cross out the 9, a 3 and 6, a 2 and 7, a 1 and 8, a 1, 3, and 5, etc. Use your calculator to help check different possible combinations.
4. If your roll is a double (e.g., two 2's), take a slip of bonus paper. (You can use any kind of counters for these bonus slips.)
5. Once a number has been crossed out, it cannot be used again. Suppose the only numbers you have left are a 3 and a 4 and your roll is 8. If you have a bonus slip, return the slip to the pile and roll again. If you do not have a bonus slip, you lose the game!

You should try to choose wisely as you cross off numbers in the first few rolls so you will not be left with numbers which are not likely (e.g., 2 and 3) or impossible (e.g., 1) to come up on their own.

2. The Crooked Calculator   SUGGESTED GRADE SPAN—4, 5

Pretend the 7, 8, and 9 keys don't work on your calculator (although 7, 8, and 9 will show on the display). Find the sums and differences below without using the 7, 8, and 9 keys. The first few in each set are easier to warm you up.

Sums	*Differences*
a) 736 + 428	a) 635 — 428
b) 294 + 583	b) 724 — 539
c) 739 + 827	c) 839 — 518
d) 789 + 987	d) 987 — 789

3. Solitaire in Spades   SUGGESTED GRADE SPAN—4, 5

Additional materials needed: Deck of cards

Object: To remove all spades from the deck in eight shuffles

Rules:
1. Shuffle the deck and turn it face down.
2. Use your calculator to keep count of the number of shuffles you have made.
3. After shuffle number 1, count off every fourth card by dealing three on one pile and the fourth on another pile. At the end of the deal remove all spades from the second pile from the deck.

4. Put all cards except the spades you removed
   back in one deck. Shuffle again. Don't forget to
   mark a 1 on your calculator. For shuffles #2–#4
   continue as you did in the first shuffle, each time
   removing the spades from the pile of every fourth
   card. (The last set in these shuffles will probably
   have less than four cards. Put the last card on
   the short pile.) Don't forget to add 1 to your
   calculator after each shuffle.
5. On shuffles #5–#8 count off every third card to
   put on the short pile.
6. At the end of the eighth shuffle see if you have
   removed all of the spades.

Variation: You can play a variation of this game with
a friend. Each player chooses a suit. Examine every
fourth card on each of five shuffles. If it is the suit
one of you has chosen, that player gets the card. At
the end of the fifth shuffle the player with the greater
number of cards in his/her suit wins.

4. **Crossword Warm-up**   SUGGESTED GRADE SPAN—4, 5

Below is a small crossword puzzle to warm up for
other word games in this chapter. First try to solve
the puzzle using only the definitions given.

Across
1. Tennis stroke
4. Seethe
5. Sinister look
6. Leave
7. Thus
9. Golly!
10. Robert E. _____
11. Diamond _____

Down
1. Fuel for the fireplace
2. Fuel for the home
3. Make holy
4. Scare word
6. Fish "lung"
8. Word of surprise
9. Congeal

If you need some help with one or more letters or words, use the problems below. Do the problem, then "flip" the calculator to read the answer.

Across
1. $238 + 569$
4. $10,000 - 2,982$
5. 5×752
6. 3×102 (Cover the first digit of your answer before flipping.)
7. 3×35 (Cover before flipping.)
9. $1,258 + 3,248$
10. $1,011 \div 3$
11. $1,000 - 283$

Down
1. $279 + 328$
2. Answer to 11 Across minus 7
3. $34,298 + 21,080$
4. 8×1001 (Cover the first digit of your answer before flipping.)
6. $10,000 - 2,284$
8. $1,000 \div 25$
9. $1,000 - 264$

Note: You may now want to try to make up crossword puzzles of your own, perhaps for friends to try. Again, first note which numbers, when flipped, look like which letters in deciding what words you can form.

5. Alphametrics   SUGGESTED GRADE SPAN—4, 5

Alphametrics are arithmetic computations which have letters in place of some or all numerals. If the same letter appears more than once in one problem, it must represent the same numeral each time.

Below are a few simple addition and subtraction alphametrics. Find the value of the letters in each. (Letter values may change in different problems.)

a)   S A V E   b)   H A V E   c)   H U R R Y
  + M O R E   + H A L F   — H O M E
  ‾‾‾‾‾‾‾‾‾‾‾   ‾‾‾‾‾‾‾‾‾‾   ‾‾‾‾‾‾‾‾‾‾‾
  M O N E Y   A L O A F   S O O N

A real challenge would be to try to make up some of your own alphametrics. The hard part is to make the letters have some message, rather than just using any letters that work.

6. A-Maze-Ing   SUGGESTED GRADE SPAN—4, 5

Object: Move through the maze, going only across or up and down, so that the sum of the numbers in the squares you pass through is the number to leave the maze. You may not go through any square twice.

Example:

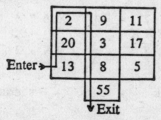

$$13 + 20 + 2 + 9 + 3 + 8 = 55$$

See if you can go through the mazes below. You may want to cover them with tracing paper as you try different paths until you find the right one.

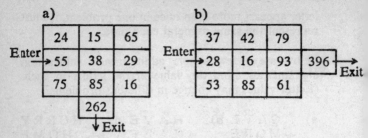

a)

24	15	65
55	38	29
75	85	16

Enter →

262

↓ Exit

b)

Enter →

37	42	79
28	16	93
53	85	61

396 → Exit

Brain-stretcher! In the maze below the enter point is not given. Try to find the correct path.

56	86	19
98	39	72
44	67	24

376 → Exit

7. X Marks the Spot   SUGGESTED GRADE SPAN—4, 5

These puzzles are somewhat like alphametrics in that you have to find missing digits. However, for these each missing digit has an "X" in its place. Use ways of reasoning "backwards" to find the missing digits.

a)
```
  X 2 X 7 1
-   X 8 X X
  ─────────
    6 2 9 3
```

b)
```
    X 6 7 4
  ×       X
  ─────────
  2 9 X 9 2
```

8. Detective Dick   SUGGESTED GRADE SPAN—5, 6

Object: First try to solve the mystery below.

In a certain supermarket the positions of cashier, manager, and butcher are held by Lois, Mary, and Nancy, but *not in that order.*

1. The butcher, who is an only child, earns the least.
2. Nancy, who married Lois' brother, earns more than the manager.

Who is the manager?

If you were not able to solve the mystery, or if you want to check your answer, do the problem below on your calculator. Then turn the display upside down. Do each problem in order as it appears in the line!

$$136,846 \div 2 - 248 \div 9 - 2,468$$

9. Stretch for 330   SUGGESTED GRADE SPAN—5, 6

Other materials: 1 card each, 2–10, from a deck of cards

Object: To get a final sum as close to 330 as possible

Rules:
1. First shuffle the 9 cards well and stack face down. Write the numbers 1–9 on a piece of paper to keep track of which you use.
2. Turn over the first card from the stack. Decide by which number 1–9 you will multiply that face value. Enter that value on your calculator. Cross out the number 1–9 by which you multiplied.
3. Turn over the next card. Select one of the 8 remaining numbers 1–9 and multiply it by the card face value. Add the result to the result in step 2. Again, cross out the number 1–9 by which you multiplied.
4. Continue this way until you've used all 9 cards and each of the multipliers 1–9. Your final sum is the sum of those 9 products.

How close did your sum come to 330? Unless you came very close, try again to get closer. See if you can figure out the strategy that will give you exactly 330!

10. More Alphametrics   SUGGESTED GRADE SPAN—5, 6

If you have not already tried game #5, read that discussion about alphametrics. Then try the problems below.

a) ```
      M A T H
    + E M A T

      I C A L
```
b)  ```
      C A R E
    - M U C H
    ---------
      L E S S
```
c) ```
      O N E
    ×   A S

    N E A T
```

**11. More X Marks the Spot**    SUGGESTED GRADE SPAN—5, 6

If you have not already tried game #7, read the discussion about this type of puzzle. Then try the problems below.

a)  ```
      X X 7, X 5 X
    ×           7
    -------------
    1, X 6 X, 1 X 1
```
b) ```
        X 2 8
    ×   X X
    ----
      1 9 X X
    X X X 0

    X X X X 8
```

**12. Calculator Crosswords**    SUGGESTED GRADE SPAN—5, 6

Below is a crossword puzzle. All words in the puzzle can be found by doing the problems shown in the "Selected Answers" section if you cannot complete
```

them otherwise. Do as much of the puzzle as you can without checking answers. If necessary, do the problems shown in the answers, then turn the display upside down for the words.

Across
1. Ear appendage
4. Not tight
8. Spanish cheer
9. Pronoun
10. ____ Abner
11. Slippery fish
13. Seep
15. Only
16. Capital of Norway
18. Wild plum

Down
1. Alluvial deposit
2. Bread spread
3. ____ of St. Mary's
4. Zodiac lion
5. Cockney pits
6. Spanish "Yes"
7. Cockney greeting
9. Washes (as a car)
12. Vend
14. Animal hotel
17. ____ and behold!

13. A-Maze-Ing B SUGGESTED GRADE SPAN—5, 6

You may want to review game #6 of this chapter for directions for solving these mazes. Then try the two below.

a)

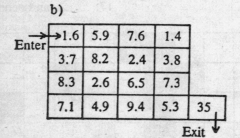

b)

1.6	5.9	7.6	1.4
3.7	8.2	2.4	3.8
8.3	2.6	6.5	7.3
7.1	4.9	9.4	5.3

Enter → →1.6 ... 35 Exit ↓

14. Scrabble Solitaire SUGGESTED GRADE SPAN—5–7

Additional Materials Needed: Scrabble game

Object: To use all the letters and get the best possible total

Rules: Form words in the same manner as when you play the game Scrabble. After each letter you insert which completes a word in one or more directions, add the total score for that round to the amount already on your calculator. (Start calculator at 0 at beginning of play.) Make choices carefully so that high-point letters are used on double- or triple-letter squares and, if possible, in double- or triple-word lines. Try to form words in such a way that these get counted more than once (often by adding an "s" on a subsequent turn). But be careful to work a pattern so that you can always form a new word. For each letter remaining at the end, if you cannot form any more words, you must subtract $5\times$ its value from the total on your calculator at that point.

Variation: You can, of course, play a regular game of Scrabble with a friend, with each of you keeping your totals on a separate calculator.

15. Traveling Salesman   SUGGESTED GRADE SPAN—6–8

The picture below represents nine cities with sales offices of the Sleep-Ease Mattress Company. You are currently in City A and have to get to City B in the shortest possible time. The numbers on the "map" show the number of hours it takes to get from one city to the next. If you can only travel from west to east (left to right) and north to south (top to bottom), what is the quickest possible time in which you can get from A to B?

Note: The directions in which you can move also imply that you cannot cut diagonally and move off the lines of map.

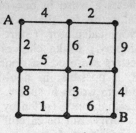

Variation: The company has just declared that they will give a bonus to the salesman who can find the shortest route from A to B which includes a total of 7 cities, counting A and B. The route must begin and end in A and B. You may travel in *any* direction on this route, but you may not pass through a city more than once. Find the shortest route which meets the requirements. Although this variation allows more direction of movement, you still cannot cut diagonally off the lines of the map.

16. Detective Dot   SUGGESTED GRADE SPAN—6–8

Object: To solve the mystery below

When Mr. Boggs, Mrs. Bless and Mr. Bliss eat out, each orders beef or chicken.

1. If Boggs orders beef, Bless orders chicken.
2. Either Boggs or Bliss orders beef, but not both.
3. Bless and Bliss do not both order chicken.

Who could have ordered beef yesterday and chicken today?

First try to solve the mystery above by logical thinking. If you are stumped, or you want to check your solution, do the problem below, then turn your display upside down.

$$99.2 - (1.1 \times 40.02)$$

17. Doubly Magic Squares

You are to complete the square below according to these directions:

1. Use the numbers 37 to 72.
2. Make the sum in the 4 × 4 square 218. (Hint— use 47–62 here.)
3. Make the sum in the 6 × 6 square 327.
4. Remember that the sum must be the same in all rows and columns and in the two main diagonals.

	60		50	70	
	53				
			40	66	

18. Calculator Crossword B

You should review #12 for general procedures. Remember to try to solve as much of the crossword as possible before using the answer key. If necessary, do the problem for any particular word, then look at the display upside down.

Across	Down
2. Nigerian tribesman	1. Superman's girlfriend
4. Do it or _____	2. One of Nixon's
6. Possessive pronoun	friends
8. Poker version	3. Civil War battle
(short spelling)	4. Island for immigrants
10. Capital of Idaho	5. Be defeated
11. Black _____ of	7. Perceive
Dakota	8. Hawaiian city
12. Stan Laurel's friend	9. Ailments
13. An exclamation	11. Boot nail
15. Person in charge	14. Greeting (slang)
16. Buckeye state	

19. Still More Alphametrics

SUGGESTED GRADE
SPAN—7–9

Review game #5 for the idea of alphametrics. Then try the puzzles below.

a)
$$\begin{array}{r} G\,E\,T \\ \times\ T\,H\,E \\ \hline S\,T\,R\,I\,K\,E \end{array}$$

b)
$$A.\,N\sqrt{.K\,O\,O\,K} = .I\,C\,E$$

(Hint: The first partial product for puzzle a) is KTGKE.)

20. Still More X Marks the Spot

SUGGESTED GRADE SPAN—7–9

Review game #7 for the idea of this type of problem. Then try the two puzzles below.

a)
```
        3 X X
        X X 2
        ─────
        X X 8
      2 X X X
    X X X 0
    ───────────
    X X X X 2 X
```

b)
```
              X X X
    X X √ X X X X 0
          1 5 2
          ─────
          X X X
          6 X X
          ─────
          X X 0
          X X 0
          ─────
```

21. A-Maze-Ing C

SUGGESTED GRADE SPAN—8, 9

Review game #6 for general procedures. Then try the two mazes below.

a)

8	−7	−9	1
−3	5	−3	−6
2	−4	10	4
−1	7	8	−2
		−9	

Enter → into −3

−9 → Exit

b)   Enter

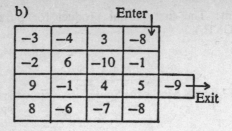

−3	−4	3	−8
−2	6	−10	−1
9	−1	4	5	−9 → Exit
8	−6	−7	−8

22. Traveling Salesman Toughie

SUGGESTED GRADE
SPAN—9 AND UP

The map below shows the 16 cities which have outlets for Hooper's Hula Hoop Company. City A is the home office and City B is the main sales branch. When setting routes, the salesman must always begin at A and end at B. The company has just announced that it will give a bonus to the salesman who can find the shortest route from A to B according to these requirements:

1. The route must include 15 cities, beginning in A; ending in B.
2. The route must pass through each city only once.
3. The route can move in any direction (left, right, up, down), but cannot go diagonally outside the lines of the "map."
4. The length of the route will be determined by adding the numbers shown on the map, representing the number of hours it takes to get from each city to the next on that line.

Can you win the bonus by finding the shortest route?

Variation: The numbers represent the number of hula hoops sold as you move along the route. Follow the same requirements as above. Can you win the bonus by finding the route that sells the most hula hoops?

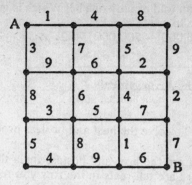

23. A Mind-Boggler

SUGGESTED GRADE
SPAN—9 AND UP

This is another mystery to solve, but much more difficult than the first two. Again, first try to reason the solution. To check your answer, or if you get stumped, do the problem at the bottom.

Clues: Joe's Supermarket was robbed by a masked bandit. Three suspects were arrested and made the statements below:

Boggle
1. I didn't do it.
2. I never saw Goggle before.
3. Sure, I knew Joe.

Goggle
1. I didn't do it.
2. Boggle and Giggle are my pals.
3. Boggle didn't do it.

Giggle
1. I didn't do it.
2. Boggle lied when he said he never saw Goggle.
3. I don't know who did it.

Each man told exactly one lie! Which is guilty?
Problem to use to check:
$([(1{,}000{,}000 - 700{,}000) \div 2] \times 3) - 70{,}091$

24. Confusing Arrangements

SUGGESTED GRADE
SPAN—9 AND UP

Object: To solve the host and hostess problems below

a) You are the host and hostess for a theater party. There are ten seats in the row you reserved. You make seating arrangements. However, when the people arrive, none of them like the seats they have. If it takes ten seconds to change to a new seating arrangement, how long might it take to try all possible arrangements to see which is preferred?

b) You have invited 12 strangers to a party. Each must shake hands with each of the others. If each handshake takes ten seconds, how much time is necessary to complete handshakes? (Do not include yourself in the handshakes.)

25. Chess Challenge

SUGGESTED GRADE
SPAN—9 AND UP

You should enjoy this challenge if you know some basic chess. Everything focuses on movement of a knight.

In the magic square below, each number 1–64 represents the position on the board reached by consecutive moves of a knight, starting in the upper left corner. There are, of course, several different ways the knight can move at each turn. The trick is to find the moves so that the numbers, when completed, form a square in which the sum of every row

and every column (but not the two diagonals!) is
260! A few numbers are already entered to help you.

1				33			18
30			3	62			
47	2						
52		4	45				
5				9			
28				24	57		
43	6						
54							11

26. You Are the Boss

SUGGESTED GRADE
SPAN—9 AND UP

Additional materials needed: 1 die

Object: You are the "boss" of the Makemoney Company. The stockholders, naturally, expect to receive
dividends each year. In fact, they expect the amount
of the dividend to be at least as much higher than the
preceding year as the cost-of-living percentage. Your
salary is the amount remaining from the profits after
the dividends are paid. Your goal is to earn at least
$50,000 this year.

Other Necessary Data:
1. total employees' salaries last year (A) $3,000,000
2. total materials costs last year (B) $500,000
3. other overhead costs last year (C) $100,000
4. total dividends paid last year (D) $1,000,000
5. total sales income last year (E) $4,600,000

Procedures:

1. On each of five rolls of the die (representing cost-of-living % computed at different times) place the face value of the die in one of the blanks below. You may choose whichever blank you wish on each roll, but once you've chosen and filled a blank, you may not change. Successive rolls are placed only in remaining blanks.

2. After inserting values in the blanks, do the computations.

3. Finally, compute $J - (F + G + H + I)$.

$$A + \underline{\quad}\% \times A = F$$
$$B + \underline{\quad}\% \times B = G$$
$$C + \underline{\quad}\% \times C = H$$
$$D + \underline{\quad}\% \times D = I$$
$$E + \underline{\quad}\% \times E = J$$

The result of step 3 is your salary (if any!) for this year. Did you earn $50,000? If not, try again. This time, try to find a general strategy to optimize your chances by making wise choices on where to place numbers as they "turn up" on rolls of the die. (But don't fudge and change choices after they're made!)

SELECTED ANSWERS

2. Below I have shown one possible way to do the problems without the 7, 8, and 9 keys. You may have found other correct ways.

Sums:
a) $636 + 100 + 426 + 2$
b) $264 + 30 + 563 + 20$
c) $636 + 103 + 626 + 201$
d) $666 + 123 + 666 + 321$

Differences:
a) 635 — 426 —2
b) 624 + 100 — 536 — 3
c) 636 + 203 — 516 —2
d) 666 + 321 — 666 — 123

4.

		L	O	B	
	B	O	I	L	
	O	G	L	E	
G	O			S	O
I		G	O	S	H
L	E	E			
L		L	I	L	

5. a)
```
   9476
 + 1086
 ------
  10562
```
O = 0   M = 1   Y = 2
A = 4   N = 5   E = 6
V = 7   R = 8   S = 9
(V and R can interchange.)

b)
```
   6190
 + 6124
 ------
  12314
```
A = 1   L = 2   O = 3
F = (can be 4, 5, 7 or 8)
H = 6   V = 9

c)
```
  10882
 — 1437
 ------
   9445
```
U = 0   H = 1   Y = 2
M = 3   O = 4   N = 5
E = 7   R = 8   S = 9

6. a) 55 + 24 + 15 + 38 + 29 + 16 + 85 = 262
b) 28 + 53 + 85 + 16 + 42 + 79 + 93 = 396
Brain-stretcher:
56 + 98 + 44 + 67 + 39 + 72 = 376

7. a)
```
    12,171
 —   5,878
 ─────────
     6,293
```

b)
```
     3,674
 ×       8
 ─────────
    29,392
```

9. You can reach 330 by adding the products 10×9, 9×8, 8×7, etc. down to 2×1. Always pick as your multiplier the value 1–9 which is one less than the face value on the card (2–10) you turn up. That will give you the maximum products, although in different order. Their sum will then be 330.

10. a)
```
   2896
 + 4289
 ──────
   7185
```
C = 1   M = 2   E = 4
L = 5   H = 6   I = 7
A = 8   T = 9

b)
```
   9805
 — 6294
 ──────
   3511
```
R = 0   S = 1   U = 2
L = 3   H = 4   E = 5
M = 6   A = 8   C = 9

c)
```
    234
 ×   15
 ──────
   3410
```
T = 0   A = 1   O = 2
N = 3   E = 4   S = 5

11. a)
```
   237,453
 ×        7
 ─────────
 1,662,171
```

b)
```
     328
 ×    56
 ──────
    1968
    1640
 ──────
   17368
```

12. Note: Some answers will have fewer letters than spaces in the puzzle. For these, clear the calculator and reenter with a 0 in front. For example, 370 (if four spaces are needed) will be entered as 0370.

Across

1. 5964 — 2157
4. 13,498 + 21,509
8. 5 × 74
9. 272 ÷ 8
10. 1,000 — 283
11. 3 × 1911
13. 50 × 64
15. 9281 — 5576
16. 4500 ÷ 6
18. 41 × 75

Down

1. 27,398 + 27,909
2. 5 × 74
3. 90,167 — 32,429
4. 296 ÷ 8
5. 9826 — 4456
6. 300 ÷ 20
7. 7 × 110 + 3
9. 27,398 + 26,106
12. 10,000 — 2265
14. (38 + 46) ÷ 42
17. (38 + 74) ÷ 16

13. a) $.5 + .3 + .1 + .9 + .3 + .9 + .8 + .2 + .6 + .4 = 5$

b) $1.6 + 3.7 + 8.2 + 2.4 + 6.5 + 7.3 + 5.3 = 35$

15.

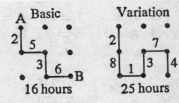

Basic	Variation
16 hours	25 hours

17.

47	60	61	50	70	39
54	57	56	51	41	68
58	53	52	55	64	45
59	48	49	62	42	67
37	71	63	69	44	43
72	38	46	40	66	65

18.

Across	Down
2. $26.9 \times .02$	1. $153.21 \div .3$
4. $.009 \times 3970$	3. $759.4 - 352.255$
6. $.2 \times 25.7$	5. 7×501
8. $.2142 \div .3$	7. $.670 \div .002$
10. $18.2 + 16.908$	8. $.2142 \div .3$
11. $90 - 32.286$	9. $2.86 + 2.911$
12. $999.99 - 682.29$	11. 4×201
13. $.04 \times 1000$	14. $.126 \div .09$
15. $.09 \times 61.2$	
16. $.084 \div .6$	

19. a)

$$\begin{array}{r} 304 \\ \times \quad 480 \\ \hline 24320 \\ 1216 \\ \hline 145920 \end{array}$$

$E = 0 \quad S = 1 \quad K = 2$
$G = 3 \quad T = 4 \quad R = 5$

b)

$$5.6\sqrt{.8008} \quad \overset{.143}{}$$

$O = 0 \quad I = 1 \quad E = 3 \quad C = 4$
$A = 5 \quad N = 6 \quad K = 8$

20. a)

$$\begin{array}{r} 394 \\ \times \quad 562 \\ \hline 788 \\ 2364 \\ 1970 \\ \hline 221428 \end{array}$$

b)

$$\begin{array}{r} 295 \\ 76\sqrt{22420} \\ 152 \\ \hline 722 \\ 684 \\ \hline 380 \\ 380 \end{array}$$

21. a) $-3 + 5 + (-7) + (-9) + 1 + (-6) + 4 + (-2) + 8 = -9$
b) $-8 + 3 + (-10) + 6 + (-2) + 9 + (-1) + 4 + (-7) + (-8) + 5 = -9$

22.

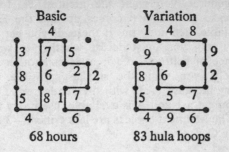

(There is another route which also gives 83. Can you find it?)

24. a) 420 days! (Take 10! for all possible seating arrangements: $10 \times 9 \times 8 \ldots \times 1$. Then multiply by 10 for total seconds. Convert to days.)

   b) 11 minutes (Find combinations of 12 things two at a time $[12 \times 11/2]$; multiply by 10 for total seconds; convert to minutes.)

25.

1	48	31	50	33	16	63	18
30	51	46	3	62	19	14	35
47	2	49	32	15	34	17	64
52	29	4	45	20	61	36	13
5	44	25	56	9	40	21	60
28	53	8	41	24	57	12	37
43	6	55	26	39	10	59	22
54	27	42	7	58	23	38	11

26. In general, you want the greatest % for income increase (E). If a 6 comes up and the E blank is available, definitely put it there. If you get a 5 in an early roll, you must decide whether to wait in the chance of getting a 6 (or at least another 5). Conversely, you want the smallest possible value for salary increase (A), with dividends next. Obviously, if you get a 1 and A is available, use it; try for a 2 in D. The best next choices are less critical—3 for B and 4 for C.

The thing that still makes this uncertain is that you can't be sure each number you want will come up. Playing the odds will help your chances, but nothing will be guaranteed.

Chapter 9

One on One

The games in this chapter are for two players. Unless indicated otherwise, only one calculator is required.

1. Tic-Tac-Toe   SUGGESTED GRADE SPAN—4–6

Additional materials needed: 3×3 grids on paper, such as

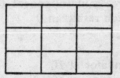

Object: To get a sum of 105 from three numbers in a row—across, down, or on a diagonal

Procedure:
1. Use the numbers 7, 14, 21, 28, 35, 42, 49, 56, and 63.
2. Players take turns inserting numbers in the grid.
3. Once a number is used, it may not be used again in the same game.
4. Use the calculator to check totals when one player gets three in any row. (You may want to mark numbers in different colors to make it easier to remember which belong to which player.)

Try to devise a strategy so that you can get at least a draw in every game.

Variation: There is an infinite variety of different kinds of numbers that can be used for this Tic-Tac-Toe. You may want to try it with the decimals .1 through .9, trying for three in a row totaling 1.5.

Try making up other variations of your own. Be careful to pick numbers and the correct "magic" total which wins the game. (A hint for picking these can be found in the "Selected Answers" for Chapter 3, #2, the "brain-stretcher.")

2. Down from Twenty   SUGGESTED GRADE SPAN—4–6

Object: To force your opponent to make the final subtraction which results in 0

Procedure:
1. Set the calculator at 20.
2. Players take turns subtracting. A player may subtract 1, 2, or 3 on each turn.
3. As the player announces what he/she will subtract, the player does so on the calculator.
4. The player who forces the opponent to make the final subtraction which results in 0 is the winner.

The game itself is easy to play. The real challenge is to try to find a strategy (as the second player) by which you will always win if the other player doesn't know it.

Variation: If both players have learned the strategy, try reversing the winning procedure. The player who makes the final subtraction is the winner, instead of the loser. How does this change the strategy?

Major variation: Once you become skilled at the strategy of this basic game and its variation you will want to try other versions for a challenge. For example, you can set the calculator at 50 and take turns subtracting 1, 2, 3, 4, 5, or 6 on each turn. You can set the calculator at 70, adding 1–8 (any of your choice) on each turn. Try to discover the winning strategies for these and similar variations. Don't forget to try the variations where the player who subtracts last is the winner.

3. 21 Pickup   SUGGESTED GRADE SPAN—4–6

Object: To force your opponent to make the final addition which results in 21

Procedure:
1. Set the calculator at 0.
2. Players take turns adding. A player may add 1, 2, or 3 on each turn.
3. As the player announces what he/she will add, the player does so on the calculator.
4. The player who forces the opponent to make the final addition which results in 21 is the winner.

This game, too, is easy to play. Again, the challenge is to find the strategy (as the second player) by which you will always win if the opponent doesn't know it.

Variation: Change the winner to the player who makes the final addition. How does this change the winning strategy?

Major variation: Once you become skilled at the strategy of this basic game and its variation, you will want to try other versions for a challenge. For example, you can set the calculator at 0 and add any of the numbers 1–10 on each turn, with the first to reach 100 as the winner. Select any number of your choice for the winning total, but alter the numbers to be added accordingly. (For 60, use 1–6, etc.) Don't forget the variation where the first to reach the number is the loser. Try to find winning strategies for each variation.

4. Nuclear Reactor   SUGGESTED GRADE SPAN—4–6

Additional materials needed: coin (any value)

Background: One player represents the director of a center which has a nuclear reactor. The second player is a spy trying to sabotage the plant. The spy tries to get the mass to go critical. The director tries to get bombardment reduced to 0 so the plant can be closed for repairs.

Object: Each player tries to reach his/her target critical count before the other: for the director, 0; the spy, 1,000,000

Rules:
1. Set the calculator at 500,000, the normal bombardment.
2. Flip the coin to see who goes first. Then take turns flipping on all successive turns.
3. If, on any flip, the coin comes up heads, the player who is the director subtracts 50,000 on the calculator. If the coin comes up tails, the spy adds 50,000.
4. The game ends when the director gets 0 or the spy gets 1,000,000.

5. Space Race   SUGGESTED GRADE SPAN—5–7

Additional materials needed: one calculator per player; pair of dice

Background: Each player represents a country which has just launched an unmanned space probe to Jupiter. Data coming back from the probes show that both have successfully escaped Earth's atmosphere at 50 miles. The race is on to be first to land on the Great Red Spot!

Object: To be the first player whose calculator exceeds the display

Rules:
1. Each player sets his/her calculator at 50.
2. Flip a coin or roll dice to see who goes first.
3. The first player rolls the dice, then multiplies the 50 on his/her display by the value on the dice, leaving the result on the display. The second player does the same for his/her turn.
4. Play continues this way, each time multiplying the value on the dice roll by the amount in the display.
5. The winner is the first player whose calculator goes beyond the display.

6. **21 Pickup B**   SUGGESTED GRADE SPAN—5–7

Additional materials needed: 21 counters (poker chips, match sticks, paper clips, etc.)

Object: To force your opponent to make the final subtraction which results in 0

Procedure:
1. Arrange the counters as shown below.

   . . . . . .
   . . . . .
   . . . .
   . . .
   . .
   .

2. Set the calculator at 21.
3. As with game #3, players will remove one, two, or three counters, doing a subtraction to match on the calculator.
4. The difference is that the player may only remove counters from a single row! That is, you cannot remove three by taking one from one row and two from another.
5. The winner is the player who forces the opponent to remove the last counter and make the final subtraction of 1, resulting in 0.

Can you find the winning strategy for this more complicated version of 21 pickup?

7. Tic-Tac-Toe B   SUGGESTED GRADE SPAN—5–7

Additional materials needed: 3×3 grids on paper (see game #1)

Object: To get three in a row (X or 0) before the opponent

Rules:
1. The first player enters any 3-digit number on the calculator.
2. The second player multiplies this by a 3-digit number of his/her choice.
3. If the answer has two digits the same (e.g., 53756), the second player can put his/her mark (either X or 0) in any empty square on the grid. If the answer has all digits different, the player makes no mark and the turn passes to the next player.
4. Play continues this way, with players alternating as the multiplier taking a turn to mark, until one player gets either three X's or three 0's in any direction to win or until all squares are filled for that game.

8. Slippery Stacks   SUGGESTED GRADE SPAN—6–8

Additional materials needed: three calculators (you may also want to use 24 counters of some type to do the game physically, as well as on the calculator)

Object: To be the player who makes the addition which results in a total of 8 on each calculator (and eight counters/pile)

Procedure: Set the calculators at 11, 7, and 6, respectively. (If you are also using counters, make piles with 11, 7, and 6.)

On each turn a number can be subtracted from one calculator and added to *one* of the others with three restrictions:

1. You cannot subtract more from a calculator than the value on the display at that turn.
2. You cannot add more to any calculator than the value on the display at that turn.
3. You cannot add the number to two calculators on the same move. (When you add to one, you must subtract from another.)

The first three moves of a sample game are shown below:

A	B	C	
11	7	6	
8	7	9	(A − 3, C + 3)
10	7	7	(C − 2, A + 2)
9	8	7	(A − 1, B + 1)

Notice that the next player can win with A − 1 and C + 1. As you play, try to find winning strategies; watch for strategies by your opponent.

9. Hit the Deck   SUGGESTED GRADE SPAN—6–8

Additional materials needed: deck of cards: three each of Ace to Nine

Object: To force your opponent to make the last subtraction, resulting in 0 on the display.

Procedure:
1. Set the calculator at 90.
2. Place the 27 cards—three Aces, three Deuces, etc. to three Nines—face up.
3. On each turn a player selects a card of his choice and subtracts its face value from the calculator (Ace = 1). That card is then removed from the set and cannot be used again. (So, for example, once nine has been subtracted three times, it cannot be subtracted again in that game.)
4. The player forced to make a subtraction resulting in 0 is the loser. A player cannot make a subtraction which gives a negative number.

Variation: Try playing with the same rules, except have the cards shuffled and in a stack face down.

10. Stretch to Sixty   SUGGESTED GRADE SPAN—6–8

Object: To be the player who makes the addition which results in 60

Procedure:
1. Set the calculator at 0.
2. The first player adds any 1-digit value 1–9.
3. On each successive turn of both players, however, the opponent must add a digit in either the same row on the face of the calculator or same column as the preceding turn of the other player. For

example, if a player adds 5, the next player must add 2 or 8 (same column) or 4 or 6 (same row). Suppose that player chooses the 8. Then the first player must choose from 7 or 9 (same row) or 2 or 5 (same column).

4. The player who is able to add a number which is *allowed* by the rules above to get 60 wins.
5. If a player on a given turn is forced by the rules to add a number which makes the sum exceed 60, subtract 25 from the value on the display at that point and continue playing.

It is difficult to devise a single strategy here, as with 7–9, because your opponent has so many choices. However, when the total reaches approximately 45, you should definitely begin planning ahead so that no matter which of the four available choices your opponent makes, he/she will allow you to make a winning choice.

11. ERA—The 27th Amendment? SUGGESTED GRADE SPAN—6–8

Additional materials needed: one calculator per player; pair of dice

Background: To amend the Constitution requires two steps. First the U.S. Congress must pass the resolution. Then the legislatures of 3/4 of the states (38 of the 50) must also ratify. Currently, although Congress has approved ERA, an insufficient number of states have ratified.

Object: To be the winning lobbyist by getting 38 (if for) or 13 (if against) states in your column of decisions

Rules:
1. Players can either agree in advance on which position they will take, or roll dice to decide which will get the choice.
2. To begin round 1, player A rolls the dice. The total shown is entered in his/her calculator as a 2-digit decimal (e.g., a roll of 6 and 5 would be entered as .11; a 2 and 4, as .06). Player A makes a second roll, multiplying the 2-digit number determined on this roll by the one already entered. The player leaves the final result on display until round 1 ends.
3. Player B takes his/her turn in the same way: two rolls, with the two 2-digit decimals being multiplied.
4. Players compare displays, focusing on the digit in the thousandths place. The player who has the greater value in this position wins the round (e.g., a display of .039 wins over .0084). Of course, if the result of one player has fewer than three decimal places, the value of the thousandths position is 0. If players have the same value in the third position, neither wins the round and play continues.
5. The player lobbying for passage wins three states each time he/she wins a round; lobbying against, one state. Play continues until the "pro" gets 38 or the "con" gets 13. The player who first attains the target number for his/her position wins.

12. Binary Brain-Stretcher

SUGGESTED GRADE
SPAN—7 AND UP

Additional materials needed: four calculators; optional—16 counters

Object: To be the player who makes the subtraction that makes all four calculators read 0 (and, if counters are used, removes the last counter or counters)

Procedure:

Set the calculators at 7, 5, 3, and 1 respectively. (If using counters, too, put them in rows of 7, 5, 3, 1.)

On each turn a player can subtract as much (remove as many counters) as he/she wishes with two restrictions:

1. A player cannot subtract more from any calculator than its total value on that turn.
2. The subtraction on any turn must all be from one calculator.

The player who can force his/her opponent to make a subtraction that gives 0 on a third calculator when two already read 0 will win by subtracting the full amount on the fourth.

A sample game is shown below:

Sample Game

	#1	#2	#3	#4
	7	5	3	1
Player A:				
Subtracts 4 from #1	3	5	3	1
Player B:				
Subtracts 4 from #2	3	1	3	1
Player A:				
Subtracts 2 from #3	3	1	1	1
Player B:				
Subtracts 2 from #1	1	1	1	1

At this point B is the sure winner, since on the next turns each must subtract 1 from one of the calculators, and B will subtract the last 1, giving 0 0 0 0.

This is really a version of the ancient game of Nim. There is an infinite number of possible variations of totals in each row which can be used. The basic strategy is the same, however, regardless of the initial totals or numbers/row.

You may not be able to figure out the winning strategy. (Hint: it is based on binary notation.) Even if you know it, however, the mental arithmetic which you must do quickly to make each move will require a lot of practice!

Variation: If you become skillful at the basic game, try a variation with three calculators (three rows of counters) set at 3, 4, and 5.

13. Calculator Baseball

SUGGESTED GRADE
SPAN—7 AND UP

Additional materials needed: three markers

Object: To have the greater number of runs scored after 9 innings

Rules: Each player, in turn, will have an inning at bat through 9 innings. Flip a coin to decide who is up first. The player who is up selects a 3-digit number at random, then passes the calculator to the other. The second player multiplies that by another 3-digit number. Based on the last 5 digits of the product, the result of that "at-bat" is determined. Possible outcomes and batting results are:

Last 5 Digits	Example	Result/Score
all the same	44444	Game over —forfeit
4 digits the same	22232	Team at bat: automatic 4 runs
3 of one digit; 2 of another	67667	Automatic 3 outs
all odd or all even —*no repeats*	31759	Home run
all odd or all even —repeats	24846	Triple
5 digits in sequence (up or down)	34567	Error— extra at-bat

3 digits the same	52585	Double
2 sets of 2 digits the same	25424	Automatic two outs
1 set of 2 digits the same	74371	Single
none of the above	18296	Out

If last digit is 1, 3, 5, 7, 9: a strike out; if last digit is 2, 4, 6, 8: a sacrifice out and all runners advance one base.

As one side reaches 3 outs, the other player goes to bat.

Man on first moves to third on a double.

Man on second moves to third on a single.

Man on second scores on a double.

It may help to keep track of runners by sketching a simple diamond like the one below. Use any handy markers as base runners. On each turn at bat, move the markers (runners) accordingly.

Variation: Use more than one player per side as teams.

Suggestion: Make up a roster of nine players per side and keep track of how each player bats. At end of game, compute batting averages.

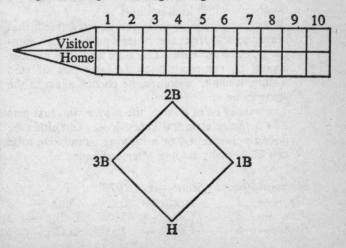

14. Hail to the Chief

Additional materials needed: one calculator per player; current list of electoral votes by state (numbers as of 1972 below)

Object: You have just been nominated by your party as the candidate for President. You must get one more than half of the electoral votes—that is, 270—to win the election (total electoral votes = 538).

Procedure:
1. Start both calculators at 0.
2. Each player enters a 5-digit number at random on his/her calculator for each turn. Each then shows the opponent his/her number, and each then divides his/her number by the one the opponent has chosen.
3. The winner for each turn is the one whose quotient has the greater value in the hundredths position of the answer. (For example, .27841 wins over .96473 because the 7 is greater than the 6—the two hundredths digits.)
4. When the winner of each turn is determined, that player selects from the states and gets that number of electoral votes. The state and vote number should be recorded; once a player has selected a state, it can't, of course, be chosen again in the same game.
5. The winner is, of course, the player who first gets 270 or more electoral votes. Votes can either be added periodically, or a running cumulative total can be kept by adding after each turn.

Electoral Votes by State—as of 1972

Ala. — 9	Ark. — 6	Conn. — 8
Alas. — 3	Cal. — 45	Del. — 3
Ariz. — 6	Colo. — 7	D.C. — 3

Fla. — 17	Minn. — 10	Ore. — 6
Ga. — 12	Miss. — 7	Pa. — 27
Haw. — 4	Mo. — 12	R.I. — 4
Ida. — 4	Mont. — 4	S.C. — 8
Ill. — 26	Neb. — 5	S.D. — 4
Ind. — 13	Nev. — 3	Tenn. — 10
Iowa — 8	N.H. — 4	Tex. — 26
Kan. — 7	N.J. — 17	Utah — 4
Ky. — 9	N.M. — 4	Vt. — 3
La. — 10	N.Y. — 41	Va. — 12
Me. — 4	N.C. — 13	Wash. — 9
Md. — 10	N.D. — 3	W.Va. — 6
Mass. — 14	Ohio — 25	Wis. — 11
Mich. — 21	Okla. — 8	Wyo. — 3

15. Settle the Strike

SUGGESTED GRADE
SPAN—7 AND UP

Additional materials needed: one calculator per player; pair of dice

Object: One player represents the company; the other, the union. The union is currently on strike because a settlement was not reached in negotiations. Each side has a limit beyond which it may not go. The winner is the player who first reaches the figure for his/her limit without exceeding it or the player who forces the other side below the strike limit.

Rules:
1. The company negotiator sets his/her calculator at 0; the union negotiator, at 800,000.
2. Company limit which player tries to reach is 350,000.
3. Union limit which player tries to reach is 450,000.
4. Danger zone is anything from 380,000 to 420,000.
5. Players take turns rolling the dice. On each turn the player mentally multiplies the total face value

of the dice by 10,000, then adds (company) or
subtracts (union) that result to the amount already on the display. (For example, if a player
rolls a 5 and 6, he/she adds or subtracts
110,000.)

6. If, on a given turn, one of the players reaches
the settlement figure for his/her side—company,
$350,000; union, $450,000—that player wins.

7. If a player's turn results in a figure in the danger
zone (380,000–420,000), the player may do the
opposite of the normal procedure (e.g., add instead of subtract). Of course, the player will have
to add the amount twice after subtracting, once
to return to the original value at the beginning
of the turn; and again, to represent the turn
itself. (See sample move #2 below.)

8. If a player's turn results in a figure on the "wrong"
side of the danger zone for him/her, the opponent
wins. The union player must avoid getting below
380,000; company, above 420,000.

Sample moves:

a) Company player has 290,000 on his/her display.
Rolls a 6. 6 × 10,000 = 60,000. 290,000 +
60,000 = 350,000. Company wins.

b) Union player has 490,000 on display. Rolls an 8.
8 × 10,000 = 80,000. 490,000 − 80,000 =
410,000 — danger zone! Player then adds 80,000
twice (once gets back to 490,000; then 490,000
+ 80,000 = 570,000). Play continues.

c) Union player has 490,000 on display. Rolls a 6.
6 × 10,000 = 60,000. 490,000 − 60,000 =
430,000. This is not the danger zone. If, on the
next turn, that player gets 6 or more, the subtraction will result in a figure less than 380,000—
the losing side of the danger zone for the union.
The company will win (unless, of course, the
company player loses just prior to that turn).
Therefore, on the next turn the player must hope
to get 5 or less to get in the danger zone and be

able to add back up to an amount greater than his/her settlement figure.

d) Company player has 330,000 on display. Rolls a 10. 10 × 10,000 = 100,000. 330,000 + 100,000 = 430,000. This is the wrong side of the danger zone for the company! Union player wins.

Variation: Play with only one die.

16. Rose Bowl Roundup   SUGGESTED GRADE
                                             SPAN—7 AND UP

Additional materials needed: one die; optional— diagram of football field and a marker for each player

Object: To have the greater point total at the end of four quarters

Rules:
1. Roll the die to determine which player goes on offense first.
2. Player A sets the calculator on 20, representing a start on the offense 20-yard line after the kick-off. He/she rolls the die. If a 1, 2, 3, or 4 comes up, the player adds 10 to the calculator. (If using diagram and marker, move to 30-yard line.) If a 5 or 6 comes up, the player subtracts 10 (move marker back to 10).
3. Player A continues his/her "quarter" in this manner until one of the following scores occurs:
   a) Player A gets 0 on calculator (marker back on own goal line)—Player B scores 2 points, a safety, and Player B goes on offense from own 20.
   b) Player A gets 70 on calculator (marker on opponent's 30) and elects to "kick a field goal" for 3 points. B then goes on offense from own 20.

c) Player A gets 70 on calculator and elects to go for a TD and extra point, scoring 7, by getting 100 on calculator. If A chooses this option, he/she must reach 100 without two successive losses of 10. If there are two successive subtractions of 10 (5 or 6 on die twice in a row), A gets no points and loses the ball. In both cases above, B then goes on offense from own 20.

When A and B complete a turn each on offense, regardless of the length of the turn in number of moves, it will be one quarter.

Players can make a simple scorecard and mark totals for each quarter (see example below).

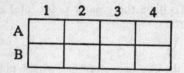

The player with the greater total at the end of four quarters is the Rose Bowl Champion.

Final Note: Games #3 and #14 from Chapter 8 can also be adapted to be two-player games. Also, any of the game-puzzles can be used as two-player games, with the winner being the player who first gets the correct solution. (Of course, this can be done only if neither has seen the solution beforehand.)

SELECTED ANSWERS

1. Be alert for combinations with a sum of 105. When your opponent has two in a row of such a combination, either block by filling in the third place with your own number or use the number your opponent needs in a different square.

2. The winning strategy for the basic game is to be sure on your turns to leave differences of 17, 13, 9, 5, and 1. For example, if you leave 5:

  a) and opponent subtracts 1 (= 4), you subtract 3 (= 1).
  b) and opponent subtracts 2 (= 3), you subtract 2 (= 1).
  c) and opponent subtracts 3 (= 2), you subtract 1 (= 1).

In each case, the opponent is forced to make the last subtraction. The winning strategy for the variations for this and other games is left for you to figure out. If you know all the winning strategies, some of the challenge will be gone.

3. The winning strategy for the basic game is to be sure on your turns to leave sums of 4, 8, 12, 16, 20. For example, if you leave 16:

  a) and opponent adds 1 (= 17), you add 3 (= 20).
  b) and opponent adds 2 (= 18), you add 2 (= 20).
  c) and opponent adds 3 (= 19), you add 1 (= 20).

In each case, the opponent must add the last 1 to get 21.

6. Always remove 4 minus the number your opponent removes from any row having at least that many in it (subtract the amount from any calculator displaying at least that much). For example, if your opponent removes 3, you remove 1.

With the exception of #11, none of the remaining games has a "sure-fire" simple winning strategy because the opponent has much freedom of choice.

With practice, however, you'll find ways to increase your chances of winning, depending on the opponent's move. The one example shown below is a "win" for game number 9.

A	B	C	
11	7	6	
17	7	0	(A + 6; C − 6) by Player A
12	12	0	(A − 5; B + 5) by Player B
8	12	4	(A − 4; C + 4) by Player A
8	8	8	(B − 4; C + 4) by Player B— Winner

12. This is a brief explanation of Nim strategy for this version.

Write the four numbers 1, 3, 5, and 7 as binary numerals; find the base 10 sum of each column. Note that all are even.

		1
	1	1
1	0	1
1	1	1
2	2	4

After each removal by your opponent, do a mental rewriting of the remaining values in binary notation and the base 10 column sums. For example, suppose your opponent removes 2 from row 2 (subtracts 2 from calculator #2). This results in 1, 1, 5, and 7, or

One column now has an odd sum. Your turn must make it even. One possibility is to change the 1 in 111 to 0. Since that 1 is in the second place, it represents subtracting 2 from the 7. Note that this gives 1, 1, 5, and 5, or:

		1
		1
1	0	1
1	0	1
2	0	4

Continue subtracting so that these column sums are always all even.

Remember I said the mental arithmetic would be difficult! If you can learn to do this quickly enough to fool your opponent, you will really be a Base 2 wizard!

Chapter 10

Three or More

All games in this chapter are for three or more players. In most cases, there is no actual limit to the number of players, except that if you get more than six, sometimes too much time elapses between turns for each player.

1. Color Calculations   SUGGESTED GRADE SPAN—4, 5

Materials needed: one calculator per player plus one extra calculator (see rules for option if no extra is available); four dice (two each of two different colors)

Object: To have the greatest total at the end of five rounds

Rules:
1. Each player sets his/her calculator at 0.
2. Players take turns rolling the dice for each of five rounds.
3. The score for each round is determined by multiplying the two 2-digit numbers formed by using the green dice as one set and the red as another. For example, suppose a player rolls and gets 2 and 6 on the green; 5 and 3 on the red. The player would calculate either:

Green		Red			
	62	×	53	= 3286	(done on
or	26	×	35	= 910	the extra
or	62	×	35	= 2170	calculator)
or	26	×	53	= 1378	

In this example, of course, the player should choose 62 × 53.

4. The player adds the result of multiplying on each turn to the amount on his/her display prior to the turn.
5. The player with the greatest total at the end of 5 rounds wins.

(If there are not enough calculators available, do all calculations for each turn for each player, keeping a record of the results on paper.)

Variations:

a) Let the green dice be tens' digits of the factors and red dice be ones' digits.
b) If players are familiar with decimal multiplication, use 6.2 × 5.3, etc.
c) Use these alternate rules: Let each dot on every die represent 10,000. From the sum of the dots on the red die, subtract the sum of the dots on the green die. For example:

red die

$$6 \times 10,000 = \quad 60,000$$
$$2 \times 10,000 = \quad \underline{20,000}$$
$$80,000$$

green die

$$5 \times 10,000 = \quad 50,000$$
$$4 \times 10,000 = \quad \underline{40,000}$$
$$90,000$$
$$80,000 - 90,000 = -10,000$$

First player to reach 500,000 or 1,000,000 wins.

2. **Join "The Juice"**   SUGGESTED GRADE SPAN—4, 5

Materials needed: one calculator per player; deck of cards; paper to record yards/player/game

Background: A premier running back in the NFL is one who gets at least 1,000 yards in a single season. O. J. Simpson, whose nickname is "The Juice," is the only runner ever to exceed 2,000 yards in a single season.

Object: To be the player with the greatest total yards at the end of the season.

Rules:
1. Shuffle cards well; deal two to each player.
2. First player shows his two cards to others. He/she then multiplies the value of the two cards: Ace through Ten are worth 1–10, respectively. Jack is 11; Queen, 12; King, 13. The product of the two values is that player's total yardage for game 1 of the NFL season (e.g., Five and Jack = 55).
3. Remaining players, in turn, follow the same procedure to get their first-game yardage. These are recorded on the score sheet.
4. Fourteen such rounds, representing the 14 games of the NFL season, are played. At the end of the 14 rounds, each player finds his total season yardage. Highest total wins.

Other Suggestions:
a) Allow players to choose names of favorite backs (e.g., Franco Harris, Larry Csonka, etc.) and use these on the score sheet.
b) Give special bonus points to players totaling over 2000 (+ 5), over 1000 (+ 2), and for winning one season title (+ 8). Play several "seasons" to get an overall bonus-point total.

3. Olympic Gold　　　SUGGESTED GRADE SPAN—5, 6

Materials needed: one calculator per player; one coin (any value); one die; optional—cut out 12 circles, four each of three different colors, and label four "gold," four "silver," and four "bronze"

Background: Olympic history was made in Women's Gymnastics in 1976 at Montreal when a 14-year-old Romanian, Nadia Comaneci, received the first perfect score (10.0) ever given in Olympic competition. Nadia went on to win the gold medal in all-around, uneven parallel bars, and balance beam, getting a total of seven perfect scores on those two pieces of apparatus. The gold for floor exercise and vault both went to Nellie Kim (U.S.S.R.), who received perfect scores in each of those events.

Object: To win the gold medal for all-around by getting the most medal points in the four events combined.

Rules:
1. Roll the die to determine order of play. Set calculators at 8.5.*
2. Player #1 begins by rolling the die and flipping the coin. The face value on the die is multiplied by .05, so the amount to be added or subtracted will be one of the six: .05, .1, .15, .2, .25, or .3. If the coin comes up heads, the player adds the amount to the number already on the calculator; if tails, he/she subtracts.
3. Remaining players, in turn, do the same thing. Play continues in this event (unevens) until one player reaches or exceeds 10.0. At that point, that player wins the gold for that event and gets 10 points for a score. (If you have made markers, give a gold.) Second high gets a silver (or 5 points); third, a bronze (or 3 points).
4. Begin the procedure again (all calculators at 8.5) for each of the remaining events: beam; vault;

---

* Top-caliber Olympic gymnasts "never" score below 8.5.

floor exercise. Give points (or medals) as in event #1.
5. The player with the highest total award points wins the all-around gold.

Variations:
a) Do six rounds, one representing each of the six men's gymnastic events: horse; vault; parallel bars; still rings; horizontal bar; floor exercise. Follow similar rules and scoring. (If "medals" are made, make six each.)
b) Require an *exact* score of 10.0 to win.

4. Disguised Display   SUGGESTED GRADE SPAN—5–7

Materials needed: one calculator per player; four dice; tape

Object: To have the lowest total on the display

Rules:
1. Set each calculator at 1000. Cover each display with masking tape, piece of paper and scotch tape, or similar covering.
2. Players #1 and #2 each roll two dice. The player whose total is greater has the choice of dividing the number on his/her calculator by that amount or telling the opponent to multiply the opponent's amount by that value.
3. Players #2 and #3 follow the same procedure. If more players than three, continue until the last player has rolled with #1; otherwise, #3 now rolls with #1.
4. Continue this procedure for four more rounds, a total of five rounds.
5. Remove the tape from each player's display. The player with the lowest total wins.

5. Emerging Nations   SUGGESTED GRADE SPAN—5–7

Materials needed: one calculator per player; pair of dice; one coin per player (any value); three players optimum; one scorecard per player (example below)

Literacy Rate	Per Capita Income	Balance of Payment

Background: Emerging nations have many problems which make it difficult for them to get a stable, but nondictatorial, government. Some factors influencing this are the per capita income, literacy rate, and balance of payment ($ exports — $ imports).

Object: To be the leader of the first emerging nation to reach a stable government

Rules:
1. Each round will consist of three different plays, one for each column on the scoreboard.
2. On play #1 each player rolls the dice. The player whose total is greatest enters .11 in the literacy column; others subtract .11.
3. On play #2 each player rolls the dice. The player whose total is greatest enters $700 in the income column; others subtract $700.
4. On play #3 each player flips a coin simultaneously. If all are the same, each enters a minus sign in the 3rd column. If two are the same and one is different, the two players with the same enter a minus sign; the third, a plus sign.
5. To stabilize the government a player must get at least .33 literacy, $2,100 income and 3 "+" in a row in balance. The first player to do this wins.

Use a calculator (or one per player, if available) to do the additions and subtractions in columns #1 and #2.

6. Fatten Your Batting Average

SUGGESTED GRADE SPAN—6–8

Materials needed: one calculator per player; pair of dice

Object: To have the highest batting average after ten games

Rules:
1. Players take turns rolling the two dice.
2. On each turn the player enters on the score sheet the lower face value under "hits" and the greater under "at-bats." (See sample score sheet below.) He/she then computes the batting average for that turn by dividing the hits by the at-bats, leaving the result on display until all players have finished that turn.
3. The player with the highest average on each turn adds 1 to the total number of hits he/she has at that point.
4. The second and all other ten rounds (games) are done in the same way, computing the average for each turn by dividing to see who has the highest.
5. At the end of ten games, however, each player adds his/her total number of hits and at-bats, dividing the first by the second. The player whose average is highest at that point is the winner and gets to play in the All-Star Game.

Sample Score Sheet

	Player A		Player B		Player C		Player D	
	H	AB	H	AB	H	AB	H	AB
#1	2	6	3	5	~~5~~	5	1	4
	(.333)		(.600)		(.800)		(.250)	

Since Player C has the highest average for this turn, he/she adds 1 to the total number of hits, giving 5.

#2   8   12   ~~7~~8   9   5   12   2   7
     (.667)   (.778)   (.417)   (.286)

Since Player B has the highest average for this turn, he/she adds 1 to the total number of hits for the turn, giving 8.

Note that the totals after two rounds (games) will be:

Player A: Hits—10   At-Bats—18
Player B: Hits—11   At-Bats—14
Player C: Hits—10   At-Bats—17
Player D: Hits— 3   At-Bats—11

7. 6-Digit Roulette   SUGGESTED GRADE SPAN—6–8

Materials needed: one calculator per player; two dice, preferably of two different colors

Object: To be the first player to reach 0

Dice code:
    Color A = digit
    Color B = place value:
    1—ones   4—thousands
    2—tens   5—ten thousands
    3—hundreds   6—hundred thousands

Rules:
1. Players each enter a 6-digit number in their calculators, using only the digits 1–6. Digits may be used more than once.
2. Players take turns rolling the dice, moving clockwise.

3. On each roll a check is made to see which players have the digit on die A in the correct place value of die B. For example, if the dice come up 3–A and 4–B, players check to see who has a 3 in the thousands' place. *All* players having this subtract 3,000 from their number.
4. The first player to reach 0 wins.

Sample Player: Original number 523614

Roll: A	B		Result	
3	4		520614	(— 3000)
1	2		520604	(— 10)
5	6		20604	(— 500000)
	etc.			

Variations:
a) When one player reaches 0, the player with the greatest total at that point wins.
b) Allow the player who rolled the dice, if he/she has the correct digit in the right place, to keep the number he/she has and require *all* other players to subtract the required value.

8. Making Your Million

SUGGESTED GRADE
SPAN—7 AND UP

Materials needed: one calculator per player; pair of dice

Object: To be the first player to become a millionaire

Rules:
1. All players start each round with a salary of $100,000. The number of rounds played will vary, and they continue until one player reaches $1,000,000.

2. Players take turns rolling the dice on each of four turns per round. Results are then added or subtracted to the amount shown on the player's display at that point.
3. The four turns for each round follow the pattern below:

Roll	Dice Total	Calculation
1	2,3,4	Reduce salary by 15%.
1	5,6,7,8	Stay even.
1	9,10,11,12	Increase salary 25%.
2	2,3,4	Buy house: — $50,000.
2	5,6,7,8	Stay even.
2	9,10,11,12	Sell house: + $75,000.
3	2,3,4	Stock loss: — $50,000.
3	5,6,7,8	Stay even.
3	9,10,11,12	Stock gain: + $75,000.
4	2,3,4	Gambling debt: — $50,000.
4	5,6,7,8	Stay even.
4	9,10,11,12	Inheritance: + $100,000.

4. At the end of each round, players record their cumulative totals for that round and any preceding rounds.
5. Calculators are set at $100,000 to begin each new round.
6. When one or more players seems likely to reach a million in a particular round, totals can be checked after each roll to see when one actually gets that amount.

9. Bicentennial Bingo

SUGGESTED GRADE
SPAN—7 AND UP

Materials needed: one calculator per player; one Bingo game (see below)

Object: To be the first player to get five markers in a row—across, down, or on a diagonal

Note: If you do not have a regular bingo game available, do the following:

1. Make at least one card per player containing a 5×5 grid and any 25 of the numbers 1–75 with 1–15 in column 1; 16–30 in column 2, etc.
2. Make 75 slips of paper, one each numbered 1–75.
3. Provide about 15 or so markers per player.

Background: The numbers 1–75 (and many beyond) can all be written by using the 4 digits of the bicentennial year 1976 once and only once with various combinations of operations, square root, exponents, decimal points, etc. In fact, most of the values can be done in more than one way! Below are shown several different possibilities for the value 90:

$$90 = 91 + 6 - 7$$
$$90 = 97 - 6 - 1$$
$$90 = 9(7 - 1)/.6$$

Rules:
1. Players take turns being "caller," pulling out a "pill" or slip and reading the number to the other players for that call.
2. When a number is read, each player who has that number on his/her card must find a combination with the 4 digits which equals the number. Allow reasonable time. Players can use scratch paper and calculators. If a player does find a correct combination, he/she writes it on separate paper hidden from others and puts a marker on the square of the Bingo card. If the player doesn't find it in time, he/she can use extra time on other turns later to do so.
3. Play continues until one player gets five in a row and can show the correct combinations for the five numbers. Replace for new game.

Variation: Rather than calling numbers, each player gets a card and tries to get five in a row for which he/she has a combination. Exchange or replace cards after each game; do not allow the same Bingo to be used again on the same card.

10. Name the Nominee

Materials needed: one calculator per player (minimum of four players suggested); deck of cards (four each of Ace through Nine); list of states and number of delegate votes (see sample below)

Object: To get 1,509 delegate votes and win your party's nomination for President

Rules:
1. A total of 4 rounds will be played.
2. For each round cards are shuffled for each turn, with four cards dealt to each player. (Take turns shuffling and dealing.)
3. On each turn each player forms two 2-digit numbers, using the face values of the cards (Ace = 1) as the digits. Each, in turn, shows the cards to other players and does the multiplication on his/her calculator, leaving the result on the display until all have completed the turn.
4. The player having the greatest product for that turn selects a state from the list and gets that number of delegate votes. This can be recorded and accumulated for each player on a separate score sheet. Once a state is chosen in a given round, it may not be selected again until a new round begins.
5. If no negotiating takes place, a round ends when one player reaches 1,509 or more votes or until

all states have been selected. At that point, scoring for the round is:

Highest — 10 (possible President)
Second — 5 (possible Vice-President)
Third — 3 (possible Secretary of State)
Fourth — 1 (possible Attorney General)
Others — 0

6. During any round, players who realize they have no chance to be first or second in totals may negotiate with the leaders to trade their votes to that point for total points for the round. If a player trades to the eventual winner of that round, he/she may trade for second, third, or fourth, whichever he/she is able to negotiate. Only if that person wins, however, does the trader get that position. If the correct person does win, the trader gets the negotiated number of points, moving all scorers from that point down a notch. For example, if a player traded to become the Vice-Presidential candidate (5 points) and the player to whom he/she traded wins the round, he/she gets the 5 points, with the actual second-highest total moving down to third; third to fourth; fourth out of the point total.

The player with the greatest number of points at the end of four such rounds is the actual Presidential nominee. Second is the Vice-Presidential nominee; etc.

DELEGATE VOTES BY STATE

Ala.	— 37	Del.	— 13	Ind.	— 76
Alas.	— 10	D.C.	— 15	Iowa	— 46
Ariz.	— 25	Fla.	— 81	Kan.	— 35
Ark.	— 27	Ga.	— 53	Ky.	— 47
Cal.	— 271	Haw.	— 17	La.	— 44
Colo.	— 36	Ida.	— 17	Me.	— 20
Conn.	— 51	Ill.	— 170	Md.	— 53

Mass. — 102	N.C. — 64	Utah — 19
Mich. — 132	N.D. — 14	Vt. — 12
Minn. — 64	Ohio — 153	Va. — 53
Miss. — 25	Okla. — 39	Wash. — 52
Mo. — 73	Ore. — 34	W.Va. — 35
Mont. — 17	Pa. — 182	Wis. — 67
Neb. — 24	R.I. — 22	Wyo. — 11
Nev. — 11	S.C. — 32	C.Z. — 3
N.H. — 18	S.D. — 17	Guam — 3
N.J. — 109	Tenn. — 49	P.Rc. — 7
N.M. — 18	Tex. — 130	V.Is. — 3
N.Y. — 278		

Total Delegate Votes — 3016
Needed to Nominate — 1509

Note: This list is from 1972. You may want to try to get the latest figures for your game.

11. Override the Veto

SUGGESTED GRADE
SPAN—7 AND UP

Materials needed: one calculator per player (two teams of two players each)

Object:
Team A is the President and his/her Congressional lobbyist. Their object is to sustain the veto by getting 1/3 + 1 of the total votes in *either* chamber: 34 in the Senate *or* 146 in the House.
Team B is the Speaker of the House and the Senate Majority Leader. Their object is to get 2/3 + 1 of the total votes in *both* chambers: 67 in the Senate *and* 291 in the House.

Rules:
1. Each player enters a 5-digit number on his/her calculator without showing the teammate for each turn.

2. The player on each team who has the number of less value then divides it by his/her teammate's number.

3. Teams examine the results of the division and score as shown:
   Team with greater digit in tenths':
   A gets 13 if greater
   B gets 34 if greater
   These points are recorded as votes in the House.
   Team with greater digit in hundredths':
   A gets 3 if greater
   B gets 8 if greater
   These points are recorded as votes in the Senate.

4. On a separate scorecard the cumulative total votes in each chamber are noted. Team A cannot do any exchanging.

5. However, once Team B exceeds the number of votes needed in one chamber, they may first shift the excess to the other. On all successive turns, however, if they win on the digit for the "filled" chamber they must only score points for the other chamber as in the scoring pattern. That is, if the House is completed first and B wins the House "digit" (tenths'), B may only add 8 to the Senate total instead of 34.

6. The team which reaches its objective first wins. That is, if Team A gets either 34 in the Senate or 146 in the House, they win. If Team B gets 67 in the Senate and 291 in the House, they win.

12. The Human Computer

SUGGESTED GRADE
SPAN—7 AND UP

Materials needed: two calculators for three players

Background: Although this is less intricate than several of the preceding games, it seems an appropriate activity with which to end the book. Calculators are, of course, a simple type of computer. We humans are the world's first (though now, probably, slowest) computer.

Object: To discover the pattern being used

Procedure: Use any procedure, or general agreement, to decide who will be #1, #2, and #3 players. Each player should copy his/her directions on a separate piece of paper, and refer only to his/her own directions.

#1: Take a calculator. Set it at 0. Say, "Start." From here on, each time you enter a number, multiply it by 3, then pass the calculator to player #2. (In this case, "0" × "3" will still be "0.")

#2: Each time #1 gives you the calculator, add 5. Write the result on paper. Then clear and return the calculator to #1. Say, "Proceed, #3."

#3: Take the other calculator (the one not yet in use). When you hear "Start," set your calculator at 0. Each time you hear "Proceed, #3," look at your calculator display. If the number there is less than 10, add 1. Tell #1 to enter the amount you now have on display on your calculator. If, instead, the number is 10, say, "Stop."

When #3 says, "Stop," look at the numbers player #2 has written. See if you can determine the pattern being used.

Note: Whether or not you know the pattern, if results come out correctly, everyone is a winner because it's more difficult than it looks for humans to act in computerlike fashion!

THE END!

Index

Ø

Fun Game Books from SIGNET

**Buy them at your local
bookstore or use coupon
on next page for ordering.**

Other SIGNET Books You'll Enjoy